Life on the Go

Devotional

for Dads

Inspiration From God for Busy Lifestyles

Life on the Go

D e v o t i o n a l

for Dads

Inspiration From God for Busy Lifestyles

By
J.M. Farro

Harrison House
Tulsa, Oklahoma

10 09 08 07 06   10 9 8 7 6 5 4 3 2 1

Life on the Go Devotional for Dads:
Inspiration From God for Busy Lifestyles
ISBN 1-57794-807-6
Copyright © 2006 By J.M. Farro
PO Box 434
Nazareth, PA 18064

Published By Harrison House, Inc.
PO Box 35035
Tulsa, Ok 74153

Contents

Introduction

Take a time-out and give your attention to the One who can give you great wisdom and inspiration for you and your family. Life may be moving fast, but when you find a few moments each day to let God impact your thoughts, your perspective will shift and those things that are weighing you down, will begin to lift. Take this powerful insight with you and as pockets of time open up, give a little to God and see the difference it will make.

You're Too Busy!

"All our busy
rushing ends
in nothing."
Psalm 39:6 NLT

I remember hearing a godly man say that if the devil can't hinder our relationship with God by making us immoral, he'll simply make us busy. All we have to do is look around us today to see the evidence of this sad truth. And where has all of our busyness gotten us? For starters, it's made us more tired. Very often, our busyness cuts into our sleep time, and when we do sleep, we don't enjoy the quality of sleep that our bodies really need. Our busy lifestyle is making us less healthy, too. We push ourselves past the point at which our bodies and minds function properly, and we often suffer for it with headaches, stomachaches, anxiety, and depression. This is not God's way. The Bible says, "A calm and undisturbed mind and heart are the life and health of the body" (Prov. 14:30 AMP). Walking in the peace that Christ died for us to have will enable us to walk in the wholeness that is His perfect will for us.

Besides costing us our health and peace of mind, busyness can cost us our God-ordained relationships. When we are feeling rushed, pressured, and preoccupied, we are destined to mistreat the people around us. As a result, our relationships with our spouses, children, parents, and friends will suffer. Most importantly, our relationship with God will suffer. If we don't spend regular, quality time with those we love—including God—our relationships will be shallow, meaningless, and unfulfilling.

The Bible indicates that we will eventually answer to God for what kept us busy while we lived on this earth. "For we must all appear and be revealed as we are before the judgment seat of Christ, so that each one may receive [his pay] according to what he has done in the body, whether good or evil [considering what his purpose and motive have been, and what he has achieved, been busy with, and given himself and his attention to accomplishing]" (2 Cor. 5:10 AMP). We must ask ourselves, "What am I giving my attention to? What keeps me busy?" And we need to ask the Lord, "What do You want me to change? What would You have me leave alone?" Jesus told His disciples, "We must work the works of Him Who sent Me and be busy with His business while it is daylight" (John 9:4 AMP). Notice that the Savior said that WE must be busy with God's business. Every child of God has an earthly assignment and purpose, and it's up to us to discover it and perform it as we walk in close fellowship with Him on a daily basis.

If you are living an overly-busy lifestyle today, the Lord is calling you to make some changes, and He doesn't expect you to make them alone. He says, "Come to Me. Get away with Me and you'll recover your life. I'll show you how to take a real rest. Walk with Me and work with Me—watch how I do it. Learn the unforced rhythms of grace" (Matt. 11:28,29 MESSAGE).

Prayer

Lord, show me how to restructure my priorities so that they will always be in line with Your will. Please don't let me live a life of busyness that will rob me of my health, my peace of mind, and my relationships. Thank You that as I give You first place in my life and live Your way, I will discover the divine destiny and fulfillment that belong to me in Christ!

The Power of God's Word

I'm convinced that if believers had a real awareness of just how powerful God's Word is, they would pay more attention to it. When Joshua was taking over Moses' job, God told him to meditate on His Word day and night. The Lord told Joshua that this was how he would be able to perform the will of God and be prosperous and successful. (Josh. 1:8.) And in Proverbs 4:20-22,

> The Word of God is full of living power. It is sharper than the sharpest knife, cutting deep into our innermost thoughts and desires.
>
> Hebrews 4:12 NLT

the Lord says that His Word is life and health to those who pay attention to it. If you're willing to invest some time and energy reading, memorizing, and meditating on the Word of God, you can experience dramatic, positive changes in every area of your life.

We can honor God by quoting and meditating on His Word three ways: (1) by putting a verse in prayer form, (2) by making it a declaration of faith, and (3) by turning it into an expression of praise. For example, each day I pray,

"Lord, order my steps this day," which is based on Psalm 37:23 (KJV). Then throughout the day I reaffirm God's answer to my prayer for guidance by declaring, "My steps are ordered by the Lord!" If doubt and fear begin to assail me, I encourage myself by praising Him for the answer with, "Thank You, Lord, that my steps are ordered by You!" If I have a need, I claim Philippians 4:19 and quote it according to my specific need. "Thank You, Lord, that You supply all my job needs!" I have used this verse to seek God for every conceivable need, including financial, healing, material, and social needs. I combine my faith with my declarations, according to Hebrews 4:2, and as a result, rest and peace flood my mind and heart. God's Word has the ability to build our faith, renew our minds, and change our hearts. If we don't meditate on God's truths day and night, we will be easy targets for Satan's deceptions. Declaring God's Word is not mind over matter—it's truth over error. Jesus used Scripture to defeat Satan when he came to tempt the Savior in the wilderness, and we can do the same thing. (Luke 4:1-12.) Each day of our lives we have two choices—we can meditate on God's promises, or we can meditate on our problems. Meditating on God's Word can bring peace, joy, life, and health. Meditating on our problems can cause anxiety, fear, despair, and sickness. The Bible tells us to "be imitators of God" (Eph. 5:1). Do you think God is wringing His hands, wondering what He's going to do about our problems? No way. The Bible says He's "watching over His Word to perform and fulfill it" on our behalf (Jer. 1:12). So let's give Him something to work with. Let's honor our God by letting Him hear His precious Word on our lips day and night, for only then will we be prosperous and successful for His glory!

Prayer

Lord, fill my heart with a growing passion for Your Word. Help me to believe, declare, and act upon it for my good and Your glory. Show me how to apply Your truth to every area of my life. Thank You, Lord, that Your Word is true and You are true to Your Word! (John 17:17; Heb. 11:11 AMP.)

Our Rightful Source

This is what the Lord says: "cursed is the one who trusts in man, who depends on flesh for his strength and whose heart turns away from the Lord…. But blessed is the man who trusts in the Lord, whose confidence is in him. He will be like a tree planted by the water that sends out its roots by the stream…."
Jeremiah 17:5,7,8

I like the way God doesn't mince words. He makes it abundantly clear that He wants us to put our trust in Him and not man. He goes so far as to say that those who put their trust in people will be cursed. Isaiah 2:22 says, "Stop trusting in man, who has but a breath in his nostrils. Of what account is he?" I especially like the way David puts it in Psalm 60:11: "Give us aid against the enemy, for the help of man is worthless." And for those of us who are tempted to put our trust in leaders, Psalm 146:3 says, "Do not put your trust in princes, in mortal men who cannot save." But the verses above reassure us that those who put their trust in God will not have to fear or worry even in a year of drought, because they will always be fresh and fruitful!

A job can be a good thing, but God doesn't want us making it our source. If we do, when we lose it, we will have no means of support. On the other hand, if we make God our provider, even if we are jobless for a time, our needs will still be met. Doctors can definitely be a blessing. But if we rely only on their limited wisdom and leave God out of the picture, it could cost us our health—maybe even our lives. Spouses and parents can be wonderful gifts, but depending on them for all our needs can be disastrous if they're ever taken from us. The good news is that God is willing and able to be all that we need in this life. If you are looking for stability and security in this ever-changing world, make our unchangeable God the source of all your needs. Then you can exclaim with the psalmist, "O Lord almighty, blessed is the man who trusts in you"! (Ps. 84:12).

Take a Break

Take time today to think about those you rely on. Would you be devastated if they were removed from your life? Reflect on Psalm 146:3. Begin to ask God to build your faith and ability to trust and rely on Him for your every need.

Cranky or Christlike?

> God wants his loved ones to get their proper rest.
> Psalm 127:2 TLB

Recently, the Lord taught me a valuable lesson about the importance of getting the proper sleep. My son had come by for a visit one evening, and we stayed up until the wee hours, watching old movies and chatting. I knew at the time that I was feeling more exhausted by the minute, but I pushed myself because I wanted to make the most of our visit together. Needless to say, the next morning I had trouble getting out of bed. Not only that, but throughout that entire day I felt irritable, negative, and extremely depressed. When I turned to the Lord in prayer and asked Him what was wrong, He dealt with me about my staying up too late the night before. At first, I had a hard time believing that the awful symptoms I was experiencing were caused by a lack of sleep. But after continuing to think and pray about it, I became fully persuaded that this was, indeed, the case.

Several days later, the Lord led me to an article written by a Christian physician who was talking about this very subject. He said that studies show that sleep deprivation can lead to high levels of irritability, stress, and negativity. He also mentioned that being robbed of sleep can hinder us from displaying the fruit of the spirit. The day that I was dragging, the last thing I felt like doing was being Christlike. I was cranky and crabby, and I wanted everyone to leave me alone.

The world's system will try to tell you that you have to work, work, work to succeed and to provide for your loved ones in this life. But that is not God's way. Scripture says, "It is vain for you to rise up early, to take rest late, to eat the bread of [anxious] toil—for he gives [blessings] to his beloved in sleep" (Ps. 127:2 AMP). The NIV footnote on this verse says, "While they sleep he provides for those he loves." Here is God's promise to His people to shower them with blessings and provisions even while they slumber.

"God wants his loved ones to get their proper rest" (Ps. 127:2 TLB). This is not only for our own sake, but for His sake and the sake of others. We will never be able to fulfill the call of God on our lives, or to impact the lives of others to our maximum potential, if we are constantly weary, stressed out, and unfocused.

for Dads

Prayer

Lord, forgive me for taking my need for the proper rest and sleep so lightly. Whenever I'm tempted to disobey You in this area, remind me of my responsibility to set a Christlike example at all times and to be prepared to minister to those around me at a moment's notice. Thank You that as I obey You in this area, my faith with be firm, my praying will be powerful, and my future will be secure in You!

Look for What God Can Do

Whenever we're experiencing trials, it's a good idea to ask the Lord how we might have caused or contributed to them in any way. If we do this with a sincere and open heart, we can depend on Him to reveal our wrongdoing. Then we can confess it, receive His forgiveness, and ask for His help not to repeat the offense. But sometimes He doesn't show us anything in particular that we have done wrong. When that's the case, we can either start dredging up all kinds of imagined offenses and focus on all the things that are wrong with us—or we can enter God's rest, keeping our eyes on Him and trusting in His willingness and ability to bring good out of the situation. Unfortunately, the last thing Satan wants is for us to rest in the Lord. More than likely, he'll bring people along our path who will begin to suggest that we must have done something wrong or we wouldn't be having these problems. Then we can start feeling guilty and condemned,

> Jesus said, "You're asking the wrong question. You're looking for someone to blame. There is no such cause-effect here. Look instead for what God can do."
> John 9:3 MESSAGE

which is exactly what the devil wanted in the first place. When there's no doubt that our own foolishness is somehow responsible for our problems, we can expect Satan to say something to us like: "You don't really expect God to help you out of this mess. After all, you brought it on by your own stupidity!" Even if that's true, it would be even more foolish not to seek or accept help from the only One who can really rescue us. While it's true that our God is a righteous Judge, it's also true that He is exceedingly merciful, especially toward those who love and reverence Him. Psalm 103:10-11 says, "He does not treat us as our sins deserve or repay us according to our iniquities. For as high as the heavens are above the earth, so great is His love for those who fear Him." And verses 14-15 NKJV assure us, "As a father pities His children, so the Lord pities those who fear Him. For He knows our frame; He remembers that we are dust." If you are in a hard place today, know that God doesn't want you spending all your time and energy trying to figure out why. That won't please or glorify Him. Instead, put your questions and regrets aside and start looking for what God can do!

Take a Break

What are you "digging" on that God wants you to leave behind? Ask Him for His help and leave those questions in the past. Begin to enter into His rest and put down your shovel today.

Our God-Given Purpose

> The Lord will fulfill his purpose for me. Psalm 138:8

I like to declare this Bible verse every day. Because I've committed my life to God, this Scripture reassures me that His purpose for my life will prevail. Many people spend years setting goals and making plans, only to discover that what they thought they wanted wasn't what they wanted at all. Nowadays, a lot of people think that getting more and more education is the answer to their search for fulfillment. Often they realize too late that all the education in the world can't guarantee they'll be truly satisfied in the end. It never occurred to them to ask God what His plans for them were. They weren't aware of the fact that He created them with a specific purpose in mind, and that if they aligned their plans with His, they would experience a peace and contentment that can be attained no other way.

If you will wholeheartedly commit your life to the Lord and cooperate with His plans for you, He will move mountains to ensure that His purpose for your life is fulfilled. You may be an artist, and people have told you there is already too much competition in the art world. The odds are stacked against you, so don't waste your time, they may say. Perhaps you're a musician, and everyone says you'd better pick another profession because there are already too many people in the music business. Maybe God has given you a vision to go into some form of ministry, but you're being told that you'll starve. Or you're feeling overwhelmed because it seems that God is leading you into the medical profession, but all you can think about are the many years and costs of education ahead of you. Listen carefully. If it's your sincere desire to fulfill your God-given purpose in life, and you believe that God is calling you into the ministry, the music business, or anywhere else——rest assured that He will make a way where there seems to be none. You will find satisfaction and joy in your labor. And no power on earth or in hell itself will be able to keep God's blessings from you!

Take a Break

What is in your heart that you've always wanted to do? What fills you with excitement and energy? Sometimes the desires in our hearts are actually placed there by God. Write those things down and commit them to prayer.

Choosing God's Best

Where is the man who fears the Lord? God will teach him how to choose the best.
Psalm 25:12 TLB

I have a sister who is unemployed right now. She's single and she has a new home, so she's understandably concerned about her situation. The other day she got an offer for a job in her field. Even though she sensed that she would be "settling" if she accepted this position, she felt obligated to go on the interview because she was in desperate need of employment. Going on the interview only convinced her even more that it was not God's best for her. I told her not to feel badly about not wanting the job, and I suggested that the Lord only sent this opportunity her way to encourage her heart. After all, she and I had been earnestly praying that God would send her some special encouragement, and perhaps that's all this job offer was meant to be. I told her that when my husband, Joe, was out of work a couple of years ago, he was most discouraged when he wasn't getting a single "lead." When he did get a lead now and then, it encouraged him greatly, because it reminded him that God had not forgotten him and that He was indeed working on his behalf. I also pointed out to my sister that we can learn a lot from job interviews, and they can help us realize what we really want in a job and what we don't. I always take great comfort in the fact that the Lord knows us better than we know ourselves, and He alone knows what we really want—we don't. I've gotten to the point now where I ask God for something, but I also make it clear to Him that if it's not His best for me, then I don't want it. Praying like this is still hard on my "flesh." But I'm learning more and more that God really does know best, and He will help us to receive His best in every situation if we will pray, do our part, and wait on Him for His perfect will and timing. Psalm 25:12 TLB says, "Where is the man who fears the Lord? God will teach him how to choose the best." Those who approach God with an attitude of trust and obedience will find that He is more than willing to help them choose His best every time.

When you're waiting upon God for something to come to pass, ask Him to send some special encouragement your way. But when He does, remember to keep praying and standing in faith for His very best!

for Dads

Take a Break

Are you settling in some areas of your life even though you know that God desires better for you? Stop wavering and choose God's best for your life. If it means utilizing self-control and abstaining from pleasures, have faith that God's best far exceeds quick satisfaction.

The Importance of Joy

Have you ever noticed how your moods can affect your whole outlook on life? When you're feeling down, it can seem like nothing's going right and everyone around you

> The joy of the Lord is your strength.
> Nehemiah 8:10

irritates you. But if you're feeling particularly cheerful one day, almost nothing bothers you. When you're filled with the joy of the Lord, you feel strong, capable, and ready for anything. That's why a joy-filled believer is hard for the devil to handle. If the enemy can steal your joy, he can rob you of almost anything, including your health.

Romans 14:17 says that the kingdom of God is "Righteousness, peace, and joy in the Holy Spirit." That should tell us just how valuable joy is to the believer. Jesus spoke about joy a lot. It was the Savior's desire that His disciples would be filled with joy. (John 16:22; 17:13.) In John 16:24, Jesus says, "Ask, using my name, and you will receive, and you will have abundant joy." And in 1 Thessalonians 5:6, Paul writes, "Be joyful always." The Bible tells us that God wants us to serve Him with joy.

Psalm 100:2 says, "Serve the Lord with gladness." And Ddeuteronomy 28:47 says that because God's people refused to serve Him joyfully, He would cause them to serve their enemies instead. The Lord deserves to have us serve Him with joy, and He's given us His Holy Spirit as our source of joy. Let me encourage you to memorize Psalm 86:4 so that the next time you need a fresh dose of joy, you can pray like David did, "Bring joy to your servant, for to you, O Lord, I lift up my soul." Before you know it, you'll be filled with the joy of the Lord, and nothing will be able to keep you down!

Prayer

Lord, I ask that by Your Spirit You would fill me with ever-lasting joy. Give me a happy heart and a cheerful mind so that I may walk in wholeness. Whenever I'm tempted to despair, remind me of the importance of joy and how You deserve a cheerful servant. Thank You that Your joy makes me strong!

The Recipe for Success

The Bible contains many promises related to the tasks we perform. The verse above is one of my favorites to pray and stand on whenever I have a job to do. Another one is Proverbs 16:3:

> Commit everything you do to the Lord. Trust him, and he will help you.
> Psalm 37:5 NLT

"Commit your work to the Lord, and then your plans will succeed." God is eager to bless the work of our hands, and He wants us to succeed in all we do. Notice, though, that He wants us to first entrust our tasks to Him. God wants to be invited into every area of our daily lives, but He is a gentleman. He will not force His help on us. That's not His style. There's a certain amount of humility involved in our asking God for help, and often it's our pride that keeps us from asking. Other times it's the belief that it's not a big enough job to seek God's help with, or it's one that we've performed countless times before. I'm familiar with that way of thinking because I used to think that way myself. Now, no matter how small or insignificant my tasks seem, I ask God for His help, and I believe it pleases Him greatly. How do I know? Because overall, my work goes more smoothly, the results are better, and I experience more joy and satisfaction.

Next time you are doing the yard work or working on your car, invite God to help you. Commit all your child care and parenting duties to Him. Don't try to raise kids these days without the divine assistance that God offers you. Don't try to drive without Him. Take the Lord along with you when you travel. And why would any child of God want to try to get through school without their heavenly Father's grace, power, and wisdom? If you're employed, bring God to your job each day, and ask Him to help you be the best employee your company's ever had. When you "Commit everything you do to the Lord," you will have at your disposal the help of the Father, Son, and Holy Spirit, as well as a legion of angels, if necessary. Today, begin seeking God's help in all your endeavors, and you can bet "The Lord your God will make you successful in everything you do"! (Deut. 30:9 NLT).

Take a Break

Purpose to seek God's help in every activity of the day. What one thing immediately comes to mind that you can commit to the Lord right now? As soon as you commit to Him, you've already begun following God's recipe for success!

The Truth About Sin

> I have been crucified with Christ and I no longer live, but Christ lives in me. The life I live in the body I live by faith in the Son of God, who loved me and gave himself for me.
>
> Galatians 2:20

Have you ever wondered why there are so many Christians today who are living lives of mediocrity instead of victory? Most likely it's because they haven't gotten a revelation of the truth of the above verses. If you have received salvation through Christ, you have been justified in the sight of God, and like the Scripture says, "If anyone is in Christ, he is a new creation; the old has gone, the new has come!" (2 Cor. 5:17). At the moment of salvation, you were changed on the inside. You were crucified with Christ, you died to the world, and you were "redeemed with the precious blood of Christ from worthless ways of living" (1 Peter 1:18). Colossians 3:3 AMP reads, "For [as far as this world is concerned] you have died, and your [new, real] life is hidden with Christ in God." Not only that, but the above verses confirm that at the time of your conversion, Christ Himself came to live on the inside of you through the Holy Spirit. But Satan wants you to believe that you're no different now than before you were saved. If he can convince you that you haven't changed on the inside, you will live a lifestyle that's not much different than a non-Christian's.

But once you get a revelation of your true identity in Christ and you walk in the light of the truth, you will no longer be a defeated Christian, but a victorious one. Once that happens you are on your way to sanctification, which is a process of growing spiritually and changing on the outside. How do we live sanctified lives in a fallen world? "By faith in the Son of God," as the verses above tell us. If you want your behavior to change so that it will be more like Christ's, then you will have to acknowledge your new identity in Christ, and you will have to resist Satan's attempts to deceive you. Of course there will be times when you sin, but the more you realize who you are in Christ, the more mature you will become spiritually and the less vulnerable you will be to temptation. First John 5:18 says, "We know that anyone born of God does not continue to sin; the one who was born of God keeps him safe, and the evil one cannot harm him." At the moment of salvation God equipped you with everything you need to live a godly life in an ungodly world. Now all you have to do is believe it. Jesus said that when we know the truth, the truth will set us free. (John 8:32.) It's my prayer that today you will begin to walk in the freedom that Christ gave His life to give you.

Prayer

Lord, Your Word says that I should "consider myself dead to sin, but alive to God in Christ Jesus" (Rom. 6:11). Help me to do that, Lord. Cause me to realize who I really am in Christ. Show me how to walk in the light of Your truth so that the enemy cannot defeat me. I want my behavior to reflect Yours, Jesus. Thank You for setting me free so that I am free indeed! (John 8:32.)

When All We Can See Are Giants!

These are the words of Joshua and Caleb after returning from their exploration of the Promised Land, along with ten other "spies" sent out by Moses, their leader. God had promised the Land of Canaan to the Israelites after he delivered them out of the hands of Pharaoh in Egypt. The Lord had told His people that the land He was giving them was lush and fertile—"a land flowing with milk and honey." When the twelve spies scouted out the land in advance, they discovered that "all the people there were of great size" (Num. 13:32), and as a result, ten of the spies brought back a "bad report." Only Joshua and Caleb declared that they were able to conquer the giants because God was on their side. And because of their

> The land we passed through and explored is exceedingly good. If the Lord is pleased with us, he will lead us into that land, a land flowing with milk and honey, and will give it to us. Only do not rebel against the Lord. And do not be afraid of the people of the land, because we will swallow them up. Their protection is gone, but the Lord is with us. Do not be afraid of them.
>
> Numbers 14:7-9

faith in God and His promises in the face of certain defeat, they were the only two spies that made it to the Promised Land.

You may have some giants looming in your life right now. They may be financial troubles or health problems, or problems with a parent, child, teacher, or boss. Maybe you've been struggling with your weight for years, and you don't see any way out. Whatever it is, remember Joshua and Caleb. When the other ten spies saw only giants, Joshua and Caleb saw God. There's a song that says, "Turn your eyes upon Jesus." If you'll do that today, God will see to it that you make it to the promised land!

Prayer

Lord, You know what I'm up against today. Sometimes my problems seem so big that all I can see is them and not You. Help me to take my eyes off the giants in my life and fix them on You. Cause me to realize how big a God You really are and how willing You are to face all my problems with me, if I'll let You. Thank You that with You beside me, the victory is mine!

Who Needs Signs?

The kings of Israel, Judah, and Edom had united to attack Moab. After a seven-day march, the army had no water left for themselves or their animals. Their situation looked hopeless, and they were prepared to die. Then good King Jehoshaphat summoned Elisha, the prophet of God, who revealed the Lord's plan to perform a miracle on their behalf. To me, the most amazing part of this prophecy is the Lord saying, "You will see neither wind nor rain…." God is saying here, "You're not going to see any signs that a miracle is coming, but it's coming just the same." And not only was God going to do something that was virtually impossible, but He said, "This is an easy thing in the eyes of the Lord"!

While the harpist was playing, the hand of the Lord came upon elisha and he said, "this is what the Lord says: make this valley full of ditches. For this is what the Lord says: you will see neither wind nor rain, yet this valley will be filled with water, and you, your cattle and your other animals will drink. This is an easy thing in the eyes of the Lord…."
2 Kings 3:16-18

for Dads

I can think of so many times that I encountered challenges in my life—and though a part of me hoped God would intervene on my behalf—my faith faltered because I thought, *I don't see any signs that He's doing anything!* Are you waiting to see some evidence that God is working on your behalf in a situation? Are you waiting for the right phone call, letter in the mail, or other tangible evidence? Rest assured that it is an easy thing for God to come to your aid, even when signs that He will do so are virtually nonexistent!

Prayer

Lord, forgive me when I've doubted You because I couldn't see any signs that You had plans to help me. Remind me that Your power and wisdom transcend my comprehension, and that Your love for me knows no bounds. Thank You that my deliverance is on its way—with or without signs!

Don't Look Back—or Ahead

Jesus makes it clear here that He doesn't want us worrying about the future. A certain amount of planning is okay, as long as it's done with God's wisdom and guidance. But worrying is another story. It's not only nonproductive, but it can be destructive, too. When Jesus prayed the Lord's prayer for His disciples, He said, "Give us this day our daily bread." Notice He didn't ask for enough bread for a year, a month, or even a week. When the Children of Israel were in the desert those forty years, God provided manna for them daily. But He gave them strict orders to gather only what they needed for that day. If they attempted to gather more, it would decay. God wants to be our provider, and He wants us to depend on His care and provision daily.

Therefore, do not worry about tomorrow, for tomorrow will worry about itself. Each day has enough trouble of its own.

Matthew 6:34

These principles don't just apply to our material needs, but to our spiritual needs as well. If you belong to the Lord and you depend on His grace to live each day, you have only the grace you need for today, whatever it may bring. You don't have the grace to live in the past. And you don't have the grace to live in the future. That's why when you live in the past, you will suffer regret and torment. And if you live in the future, you will be plagued with anxiety and fear. Eventually, your mind and body will pay the price. But if you live each day depending on God and His provision and grace, you will experience an inner peace and joy, no matter what the circumstances. Instead of looking ahead or behind, look up into the blessed face of the Savior—and He will make your cup overflow!

Prayer

Lord, help me not to live in the past or worry about tomorrow. Give me the grace I need each day to face all my responsibilities and challenges with confidence and courage. Teach me how to depend on You and trust in You so that I'll never have to be fearful of what the future may bring. Thank You that You're all I'll ever need!

Grace for the Guilty

King Jehoshaphat was king of Judah, and he had a heart for God. But he unwisely made an alliance with evil king Ahab of Israel. When their armies attacked the Arameans, Ahab shrewdly disguised himself, while insisting that Jehoshaphat wear his royal robes. Consequently, the Arameans—who were ordered to kill only the king of Israel—mistook Jehoshaphat for Ahab, and they tried to kill him. Jehoshaphat cried out to the Lord, who saved His servant from destruction.

This message is good news today for those of us who have a heart for God but sometimes miss the mark. Are you in financial trouble today because of poor planning or foolish spending? Did you get involved in a relationship that was out of God's will for

> Now the king of Aram had ordered his chariot commanders, "Do not fight with anyone, small or great, except the king of Israel." When the chariot commanders saw Jehoshaphat, they thought, "This is the king of Israel." So they turned to attack him, but Jehoshaphat cried out, and the Lord helped him.
>
> 2 Chronicles 18:30,31

you? Are you overweight today because of poor eating habits? Maybe you've adopted the attitude, "I've made my bed, now I'll have to lie in it." You may feel like you deserve to suffer the consequences of your mistake, and you don't even feel like you can ask God for help. Jehoshaphat made a terrible mistake, but when faced with the consequences of his actions, he cried out to God and was rescued. No matter how great your sin, turn to the Lord today and receive His mercy and grace. In John chapter 9 of the *Message Bible,* Jesus speaks some words which I pray will be a comfort to you: "You're looking for someone to blame.... Look instead for what God can do"!

Take a Break

Do you feel that you've missed the mark in some way? It's so important to look instead at what God can do! Search God's word today for Scriptures that will infuse you with strength to forge a better path.

Pursuing Peace in Our Families

If you're tired of the strife in your family and you want it to change, I can tell you from experience that you can make a difference. But you've got to be committed, and you've got to rely on God's grace,

> Without wood a
> fire goes out;
> without gossip a
> quarrel dies down.
> Proverbs 26:20

because the devil isn't going to make it easy for you. Satan is determined to create strife and division in our families because he knows that the fullness of God's blessings are bestowed upon those who dwell in unity and harmony. (Ps. 133:1,3.) He also knows that "a home filled with argument and strife is doomed" (Luke 11:17 TLB). But if you are a child of God, you are equipped with Holy Spirit power to overcome the enemy's schemes. The Bible tells us to "work hard at living in peace with others" (Ps. 34:14; 1 Peter 3:11 NLT). If you're serious about wanting peace in your family, you're going to have to work hard at it. You're going to have to "make allowance for each other's faults and forgive the person who offends you." If you can't do it for any other reason, then do it simply because "the Lord forgave you" (Col. 3:13 NLT). When it's absolutely necessary to confront a family member about their behavior, don't talk about them behind their back, but "speak the truth in love" (Eph. 4:15). Make an effort to speak only words that encourage, build up, and benefit others. (Eph. 4:29.) And pray for your family. Your prayers can move the mighty hand of God in awesome ways. Rest assured that the Lord will honor you for your faithfulness, obedience, and love. My prayer for you is that today you'll take the first step toward bringing healing to your household and discover for yourself the heavenly rewards of a family dwelling in peace!

Prayer

Lord, give me a holy determination to initiate healing in my household, and show me how to take the first step. When I'm tempted to participate in behavior that produces strife, remind me that I have the Holy Spirit power to make a difference. Make me quick to forgive and help me to always speak the truth in love. Thank you for blessing my family with peace and harmony as a result!

Praise in the Midst of Problems

The Bible says that David was a man after God's own heart. (Acts 13:22.) One reason for that was his willingness to praise God in the darkest of times. Scripture reveals that after his first child with Bathsheba died, he went straight to the temple to worship the Lord. (2 Sam. 12:20.) David knew that no matter what was going on in his life, God was still worthy of his devotion and praise. In Psalm 34:1, he writes, "I will bless the Lord at all times; his praise shall continually be in my mouth." I especially like the way the *Living Bible* puts it: "I will praise the Lord no matter what happens." And even though David was a mighty warrior who often relied on weapons of war for his defense, he also knew that praise was an important weapon in his arsenal. In Psalm 18:3, he writes, "I will call upon the Lord, who is worthy to be praised, so shall I be saved from my enemies." If you are going through some difficult times right now, don't despair. Begin right now to sing praises to

> I will bless the Lord at all times; his praise shall continually be in my mouth.
> Psalm 34:1 NASB

the Lord and discover for yourself the peace, joy, and victory that a praise-filled heart can bring!

Take a Break

Praising God can be a life-changing act. Buy a good praise and worship CD and begin praising God as you drive to work or while you are working around the house. Allow the words to sink into your mind and spirit. Before you know it, you will be singing praises unto God throughout your day.

You Have a Job To Do

When Jesus told the parable of the talents, He was letting us know that each of us has a special purpose in life, and God expects us to cooperate with Him so that it is fulfilled. All three servants in the parable are given various talents, which represent the individual's gifts and resources. The servants who put their gifts to good use and were productive were rewarded by the master. They were given more resources and greater responsibility. But one of the servants was so fearful and self-centered that he buried his talent and was totally unfruitful for the master. Jesus calls him a "worthless servant." If you are a child of God, He has blessed you with special gifts that He expects you to use for His glory. If you don't know what they are, ask Him to reveal them to you. Ephesians 5:15 AMP says that we should "live purposefully" and make the most of our time. You have a job to do! There may be people in this world right now who will never receive

> For we are God's workmanship, created in christ Jesus to do good works, which God prepared in advance for us to do.
> Ephesians 2:10

the gift of salvation unless you take your place in the Body of Christ. It's my heartfelt prayer that you will make a decision today to cooperate with God's plan for your life and align your will with His. If you do, God's promise in Psalm 138:8 belongs to you: "The Lord will fulfill his purpose for me"!

Prayer

Lord, today I commit to You all that I am and all that I have, and I ask that You fulfill Your purpose for my life. Show me what my gifts are and help me to use them for Your glory. Use me to lead others to You. The next time I doubt that my life has a special purpose, remind me of the truth. Thank You that You will fulfill Your purpose for me and that You will be glorified!

Our "Unrewarded" Work

Have you ever had days when you questioned why you were so committed to living the Christian life, doing the Lord's work? I have. Sometimes you look around and all you can see are people living for themselves, instead of the Lord. Many times it looks like unbelievers are being blessed more than we are. But I think what's the most disheartening is seeing so many Christians living mediocre lives. I'm referring to believers who go to church on Sunday, and maybe even are active in the church, but live lives devoid of a real passion for God. Often these same people look at you like you're some sort of fanatic because you aren't satisfied having a superficial relationship

There is going to come a time of testing at the judgment day to see what kind of work each builder has done. Everyone's work will be put through the fire to see whether or not it keeps its value. If the work survives the fire, that builder will receive a reward. But if the work is burned up, the builder will suffer great loss. The builders themselves will be saved, but like someone escaping through a wall of flames.

1 Corinthians 3:13-15 NLT

with God. Sometimes it's enough to make you want to scream—or cry.

I love the verses at the beginning of this devotion by the Apostle Paul. They remind me that when we get to heaven, all the things we did here out of love for the Lord will finally be rewarded. On the other hand, those believers who served themselves or served God with wrong motives will find that their rewards will not follow them into heaven. They themselves will be saved, but they'll have nothing to show for their lives after they leave here. But those of us who gave of our time and ourselves, often with little or no earthly reward, will find an abundance of heavenly rewards waiting for us. Remember all those prayers you prayed when no one knew except you and God? What about all those times you said "no" to yourself when everyone else was doing what they pleased? And how about all the time you spent serving others, without ever seeing a single penny for it? Think of all the things you've done—or not done—out of love for the Lord that earned you little or no recognition or reward here on earth. These are the things that God holds closest to His heart. They are the very things that will bring you the greatest rewards from Him when you reach your heavenly home. And now I encourage you to "always give yourselves fully to the work of the Lord, because you know that your labor in the Lord is not in vain"! (1 Cor. 15:58).

Take a Break

Look for an opportunity today to anonymously bless someone. Seek out 2-3 chances to secretly serve God where you will receive no recognition. Reflect on the reward of serving God rather than man.

Waiting for God's Best

> Yet the Lord longs to be gracious to you; he rises to show you compassion. For the Lord is a God of justice. Blessed are all who wait for him!
> Isaiah 30:18

Sometimes it seems that God has put us on a shelf. It can be bewildering, frustrating, and depressing. We have a hard time trying to imagine any good coming out of it. One of the hardest parts is having to face all of the well-meaning people who keep saying, "What are you going to do?" You feel like you've done all that you can do. But that doesn't stop you from trying to come up with something. Then it occurs to you that maybe there's a way you can "help God." And you try to think of ways to "make something happen." Listen. If you really want to help God—trust Him. When He makes you wait, there's a good reason for it. The fact is, there are some blessings we are never going to receive unless we wait for them. Yes, these times of waiting are uncomfortable for us. Sometimes they're downright painful. But if we try to make our own way instead of waiting on God, we will miss out on God's best for us. Let me encourage you today with some words from a man who had to do a lot of waiting in his life, but who was blessed beyond belief. In Psalm 27:14, David says, "Wait for the Lord; be strong and take heart, and wait for the Lord"!

Prayer

Lord, You know how hard waiting is for me. Please give me the patience I need to wait for Your perfect timing in everything. Help me not to settle for second best. When I'm tempted to "make something happen," speak to my heart and remind me what my impatience can cost me. Help me to not only wait, but to do so with a good attitude. Thank You for all the blessings You have in store for me!

My Father Is Greater Than All

> My father, who has given them to me, is greater than all.
> John 10:29

If you have put your hope in Christ, then you have been equipped with heavenly weapons to be an overcomer. I urge you to make a commitment to dig into God's Word and discover for yourself how the Lord has provided you with everything you need to walk in victory. The Apostle John reminds us that because we have been born of God, the One who lives in us (God) is greater than the one who is in the world (Satan). (1 John 4:4.) And Paul reminds us that the Lord is not neutral when he writes, "If God is for us, who can be against us?" (Rom. 8:31). On our own we can do nothing. (John 15:5.) But with God on our side, "we are more than conquerors" (Rom. 8:37).

It's true that Satan is a formidable opponent. But he's no match for God. When we fear the devil and concentrate on his activities, we actually play into his hands and give him the kind of attention and control he thrives on. But when we keep our eyes on God and attend to His Word, we strengthen our defenses against satanic attack.

The next time you are in a trial and are feeling "under attack," make a conscious decision to focus not on the devil's destructiveness, but on God's greatness. Take heart and remember the Savior's words—your Father is greater than all!

Take a Break

Write down all the trials you are facing today on a sheet of paper. Beside each one, write out a Scripture to stand on for that particular situation. Keep that piece of paper where you can see it every day, and focus on what God's Word promises instead of the trial.

God's Perfect Plan for Us

"for I know the plans I have for you," declares the Lord, "plans to prosper you and not to harm you, plans to give you hope and a future."
Jeremiah 29:11

Ephesians 2:10 says, "For we are God's workmanship, created in Christ Jesus to do good works, which God prepared in advance for us to do." When God designed you, He equipped you with everything you would need to fulfill your God-given purpose. He's given you gifts and skills that He wants to help you develop over the course of your life. If you ask Him what they are, He'll show you. He may direct you to get some special education or training, or He may not. The key to fulfilling your God-given call is to seek the Lord daily. Don't wait until you're at a crossroads in your life, having to make an important decision that will affect your whole future. If you do, chances are that you will significantly delay receiving the rich rewards God has in store for you. Hebrews 11:6 says, "You can never please God without faith, without depending on him. Anyone who wants to come to God must believe that there is a God and that he rewards those who sincerely look for him." If you live your life depending on God's wisdom, guidance, and grace daily, you can count on Him to lead you in the path of His greatest blessings. The truth is that there is no way for us to improve on God's perfect plan for our lives. The sooner we get a hold of this truth, the sooner we can begin cooperating with Him to bring it to pass in our lives—and the sooner we can begin reaping His blessed rewards!

Take a Break

Write down your dreams. Commit them to God. Ask Him to speak to you His vision and direction for your life.

Friendships According to God

> The righteous should choose his friends carefully, for the way of the wicked leads them astray.
>
> Proverbs 12:26 NKJV

What kind of friends does God want us to have? The Psalmist tells us in Psalm 119:63 NKJV, "I am a companion of all those who fear you, and of those who keep your precepts." Our closest friends should love the Lord and seek to please Him. If your closest companions are not believers, you are out of God's will, and you need to seek the Lord and ask Him how to separate yourself from these associations. I know from experience that He will show you how. When I first began getting serious about my relationship with the Lord, I had some close friends who did not know God. Some of these friendships were decades old, and it grieved my heart to think of ending them. But after seeking God's wisdom and guidance, I put these relationships on the altar and asked Him to help me sever these ties in a way that would please and glorify Him. I won't say that it wasn't painful or difficult for me at times, but I must tell you that the Lord gave me a peace and reassurance that I still can't explain. If you don't have some close believing friends, then you need to earnestly ask God for some. But keep in mind that He may not answer your prayer until you step out in faith and begin distancing yourself from any unbelieving companions you have in your life right now. You may even have to endure a period of loneliness. If you do, you will have the opportunity to prove to God, yourself, and others that you are serious about pleasing Him in this area. And the Lord will reward you with new and exciting "divine connections" that will bless you and bring you closer to Him. If you are a child of the King, you don't ever have to feel lonely or abandoned. Jesus Himself said, "I will not abandon you as orphans—I will come to you" (John 14:18 NLT). And He wants to be your closest friend. (John 15:15.) Today, open up your heart and let the Savior be to you all that He longs to be, and experience for yourself true friendship at its best!

Take a Break

Examine your relationships with your close friends. Are they a godly influence? If not, begin to distance yourself and ask God to help you sever your ties with them. Pray that God will send you good Christian friends.

for Dads

Step Out in Faith

During the fourth watch of the night Jesus went out to them, walking on the lake. When the disciples saw him walking on the lake, they were terrified. It's a ghost," they said, and cried out in fear. But Jesus immediately said to them: "take courage! It is I. Don't be afraid." "Lord, if it's you," peter replied, "tell me to come to you on the water." "come," he said. Then peter got down out of the boat, walked on the water and came toward Jesus. But when he saw the wind, he was afraid and, beginning to sink, cried out, "Lord, save me!" Immediately Jesus reached out his hand and caught him. "you of little faith," he said, "why did you doubt?"

Matthew 14:25-31

Peter was actually walking on the water until he looked around and noticed the wind and the waves. Then he began to sink. Likewise, when we go through troubled times, if we focus on the circumstances surrounding us, we too will become fearful and sink. But if we keep our eyes on Jesus and focus on His ability and willingness to carry us through, we will eventually come out on top. Notice that when Peter began to focus on the commotion about him, which caused him to sink, Jesus chided him for a lack of faith.

While it's God who helps us to overcome our adversities, it's our faith that opens the door to receive His help.

But there's another interesting lesson for us here. Peter was the only disciple who had the courage to get out of the boat! Yes, he took his eyes off Jesus and began to sink as a result. Still, he was the only disciple to experience the miracle of walking on water with the Master. If you are going to do anything substantial for God, there are going to be times when He beckons you to get out of the boat and step out in faith. That means leaving your safety zone behind. It also means taking some risks. If you're waiting for the water to come inside the boat before you'll walk on it, you can forget it. God will not force you to get out of the boat. But if He calls and you don't answer, you will never know what awesome things He had planned for you. If you feel that the Lord is asking you today to step out in faith, tell Him you want His direction and timing, and ask Him to give you the courage you need to do His will. Then prepare to step out of the boat and into God's glory!

Prayer

Lord, when I go through trials, help me to keep my eyes off my circumstances and on You. Hold me up and guide me safely through the storms of life. Whenever You call me to step out in faith, give me Your direction, discernment, and courage. Help me to be bold but not foolhardy. Help me to never jump ahead of Your plan or lag behind. Thank You for making me an overcomer and an instrument for Your glory!

Don't Push!

Sometimes doing nothing in a situation is the hardest thing for us to do. But, often, it's the best thing. Sometimes it's easier for us to hear "no" than to hear "wait." But the

> "Cease striving and know that I am God."
> Psalm 46:10 NASB

truth is that there are some blessings in this life that we can never receive until we go through a period of waiting. Why does the Lord keep us waiting sometimes? There could be many reasons, some of which we may never know or understand. In some cases, God needs to do a work in our hearts and lives before He can provide the answer to our prayers. It may be that the Lord will not change our circumstances until our circumstances change us. Sometimes we are kept waiting because God is in the process of orchestrating events, or changing people's minds. What we have to remember is that the Lord does a lot of His best work behind the scenes, and just because we don't see anything happening, doesn't mean that it's not. God knows that these waiting periods stretch and strengthen our faith, and that they prepare us for the extraordinary blessings that He has in store for us. The worst thing we could possibly do is to try to control or manipulate circumstances, so that we end up violating God's perfect will and timing. That would only cause us pain, loss, and disappointment.

The truth is that we're going to spend more of our lives waiting on God than we are receiving from Him. That's why the Bible says, "Wait on your God continually" (Hosea 12:6 NKJV). But how we wait is important to the Lord, and can greatly affect our outcome. Lamentations 3:25 (AMP) says, "The Lord is good to those who hopefully and expectantly wait for him." While we're waiting for the Lord to intervene, we are to wait with expectant hearts, knowing that as long as we're praying and believing, He is busy working on our behalf. We must keep in mind that Satan will do his best to make our circumstances look worse than they really are. He will try to fill us with fear in order to get us to do something hasty and outside the will of God. He wants more than anything for us to miss out on God's best, because it's in God's perfect will where we will be the most fruitful, successful, and blessed—and where we'll be the greatest threat to his kingdom of darkness.

May this word from the Lord challenge and inspire you today—"Don't be impatient for the Lord to act!

Keep traveling steadily along His pathway and in due season He will honor you with every blessing" (Psalm 37:34 TLB)!

Prayer

Lord, when I'm about to do something hasty or foolish, let me hear Your voice telling me, "Don't push!" Teach me how to seek You each day through prayer, praise, and the reading of Your Word. Thank You that as I wait upon You in faith, I will reap an abundance of blessings, instead of regrets!

Encouragement for the Faithful

Yet I reserve seven thousand in israel—all whose knees have not bowed down to baal and all whose mouths have not kissed him.

1 Kings 19:18

These comforting words were spoken by God to the great prophet Elijah. At the time Elijah was feeling sorry for himself and lamenting the fact that he was the only one left in Israel who was true to God. The Lord sets the prophet straight by reassuring him that a faithful remnant still exists in the land, and Elijah is not alone.

I often hear from believers who are feeling downhearted and discouraged because of all the people around them who profess to be Christians but who are living carnal, worldly lives. If you're one of these faithful ones, I have some encouraging news for you today. Just like there existed a faithful remnant in Elijah's time, there exists one today. The Apostle Paul writes about it in Romans 11:2-5, where he says, "So too, at the present time there is a remnant chosen by grace" (v. 5).

Even though we are not alone in serving the Lord faithfully, we will feel alone sometimes. That's when we need to heed some practical advice from the Bible so that we won't lose heart or be tempted to backslide. The author of Hebrews writes, "Let us run with perseverance the race marked out for us. Let us fix our eyes on Jesus, the author and perfecter of our faith" (Heb. 12:1,2). If we don't keep our eyes on the Lord, and if we let our eyes shift to focusing on other believers—especially carnal ones—we can risk becoming doubtful and discouraged. That's exactly what the enemy of our souls, Satan, wants. He will parade all kinds of Christians before us who are living sloppy lives. And he will try to convince us that the Christian life is simply too hard and that God is expecting too much from us. Yes, it's true that trying to live a Christlike life can be hard. But those of us who have learned the hard way could attest to the fact that living our lives apart from Christ is even harder. Besides that, God has given us the Holy Spirit so that we can follow Jesus and become more like Him each day, as we devote ourselves to Him and His Word.

Prayer

Lord, forgive me for the times I've gotten distracted and discouraged by the behavior of other Christians. I pray that from now on their conduct will create in me a new resolve to devote myself to You and Your ways more and more. Thank You that my continued faithfulness will prove Your promises true!

Believe and Receive

These verses are a great encouragement to those of us who have ever had to endure long periods of waiting before we saw the fulfillment of God's promises to us. The emphasis here is upon the fact that Abraham's situation was completely hopeless. Yet he believed God's promise to give him a son in his old age. It was many years before God fulfilled this promise to Abraham, and he made some mistakes during those years. Still, these verses don't mention Abraham's doubts but focus instead on his faith. That fact should encourage us, too. Though we may struggle with our own doubts from time to time, if we hold

Against all hope, abraham in hope believed and so became the father of many nations, just as it had been said to him, "so shall your offspring be." Without weakening in his faith, he faced the fact that his body was as good as dead—since he was about a hundred years old—and that sarah's womb was also dead. Yet he did not waver through unbelief regarding the promise of God, but was strengthened in his faith and gave glory to God, being fully persuaded that God had power to do what he had promised.

Romans 4:18-21

on to God's promises, we will receive our reward just as Abraham did.

If you are not feeling very hopeful today that God's promises to you will ever come to pass, I urge you to hold on to your faith. Look at these verses in Hebrews 10:35-36 NLT: "Do not throw away this confident trust in the Lord, no matter what happens. Remember the great reward it brings you! Patient endurance is what you need now, so you will continue to do God's will. Then you will receive all that He has promised." If you throw your faith away before God fulfills His promises to you, you will never receive the reward He has waiting for you. Ask the Lord to give you the patience and endurance you need to stand strong, then do your part by hanging in there when the going gets tough. Hebrews 6:12 TLB says, "Be anxious to follow the example of those who receive all that God has promised them because of their strong faith and patience." Follow Abraham's example and receive all that the Lord has promised you. Not only will you be blessed, but God will be glorified through you, and then you can be an example to someone else whose faith is faltering.

Take a Break

Whether you feel like it or not, whether your faith is on the brink of faltering or you are standing strong, lift your hands even now and offer thanksgiving and praise to the One who always keeps His promise of victory to those who trust Him.

Handling Finances God's Way

> Of what use is money in the hand of a fool, since he has no desire to get wisdom?
> Proverbs 17:16

A few years ago, when I became serious about getting out of debt, the Lord began showing me this verse. While it was His desire for me to live free from burdensome debt, He wasn't inclined to give me much help until I got serious about seeking His wisdom for handling my finances. He taught me a few things that have made all the difference, and I'd like to share them with you.

First, we have to seek God's wisdom and His will concerning our finances. If there's something we want—like a newer car or a vacation—we need to consult Him before we decide to take action. If we're not sure we have the Lord's permission, we need to wait on Him. And waiting on God is the second important thing He taught me. Each time I buy something on credit without God's approval, I forfeit the opportunity for Him to provide it for me debt-free. I've gotten to the point where I'm willing to wait on God for things if it means I can eventually pay cash for them. When you're serious enough about getting out of debt to do that, God will work wonders in your finances. Third, we need to trust God's provision. He has promised to abundantly supply all our needs (Phil. 4:19), and when we don't trust Him to do so, He takes it personally. God doesn't want us panicking when unexpected expenses come up. He also doesn't want us to be materialistic or self-indulgent. God wants to indulge us from time to time, but only if we don't continually indulge ourselves. Jesus told us to seek first God's kingdom and righteousness, and then He would supply our material needs. (Matt. 6:33.) He also equated those who seek things with pagans. The bottom line is that believers are not to seek things—we are to seek God. Then God will meet all our needs.

If you've made some mistakes with your finances, confess poor stewardship to the Lord and ask Him to help you be the steward He wants you to be. And know that God means it when He says, "Those who seek the Lord lack no good thing"! (Ps. 34:10).

Take a Break

Take the following action steps concerning your financial situation today:

1. Seek God's wisdom and will.

2. Wait on God's timing.

3. Trust God's provision.

Take Heart—You Are Not Alone

These are just a few of the verses in the Bible that let us know that we can expect to go through some difficult times while we're on this earth. The good news is, though, that God will be with us so that we will not have to go through them alone. Some Christians seem to think that we shouldn't have to experience trials in this life and that we should expect God to spare us from them all. Then there are those believers who think that we shouldn't pray for protection or deliverance from suffering, because it's our lot in life to suffer. But the Bible is filled with numerous accounts of God miraculously delivering His people from all kinds of tribulations. It's also filled with promises of protection for believers. Just take a look

Do not be afraid, for I have ransomed you. I have called you by name; you are mine. When you go through deep waters and great trouble, I will be with you. When you go through rivers of difficulty, you will not drown! When you walk through the fire of oppression, you will not be burned up; the flames will not consume you. For I am the Lord, your God, the Holy One of Israel, your Savior.

Isaiah 43:1-3 NLT

at Psalm 91, one of the most quoted Bible passages of all time. As children of God we have the privilege, even the obligation at times, to pray for protection from evil and harm—not just for ourselves, but for others. While prayers like these will not always be answered the way we expect, we will always be worse off without them.

It is my heartfelt prayer that you would be spared from all difficulties in this life. But since that's not very likely, let me encourage you with some promises from God's Word which will reassure you that God will not abandon you during these times. Psalm 23:4 says, "Even though I walk through the valley of the shadow of death, I will fear no evil, for you are with me; your rod and your staff, they comfort me." David knew the Lord would never forsake him in times of trouble, and neither will He forsake you. In John 16:33 TLB, Jesus warns us to expect difficult times while we're here, and at the same time, He comforts us: "Here on earth you will have many trials and sorrows; but cheer up, for I have overcome the world." If you are in a trial today, please know that God has not left you alone in your time of need. If you are in doubt, ask Him to reveal Himself and His unfailing love for you. You may be surprised how quickly He answers that prayer. Let me encourage you today with Psalm 34:19 TLB: "The good man does not escape all troubles—he has them too. But the Lord helps him in each and every one"!

Prayer

Lord, sometimes when I go through difficult times I feel so alone and helpless. At those times I ask that You wrap Your arms of love around me and comfort me the way only You can. Let me feel Your presence in a special way, and lift me above my circumstances. Thank You that You will never leave me nor forsake me!

No Condemnation

"Neither do I condemn you," Jesus declared. "Go now and leave your life of sin."
John 8:11

If you've ever struggled with guilt and condemnation as I have, the above verse is for you as much as it is for me. The Apostle John records that when a woman caught in the act of adultery was brought before Jesus, instead of condemning her, He forgave her. During biblical times, according to Jewish law, people were stoned to death for this sin, so the Master's act of forgiveness here is truly remarkable. This passage should be a great comfort to all of us who have suffered the torment of guilt and condemnation after we've sinned. Jesus said, "Whoever believes in [Me] is not condemned, but whoever does not believe stands condemned already because he has not believed in the name of God's one and only Son" (John 3:18). And in John 5:24, Jesus says, "I tell you the truth, whoever hears my word and believes him who sent me has eternal life and will not be condemned; he has crossed over from death to life." These two statements make it clear that because we made the decision to put our faith in Christ and accept Him as our personal

Savior, we will escape God's judgment and condemnation. We are not condemned because Jesus was condemned on our behalf on the cross. (Rom. 8:1.)

One thing we have to keep reminding ourselves is that God does not condemn the believer. While He gives us His Holy Spirit, whose job it is to convict us of sin so that we'll confess it and repent of it, the truth is that condemnation comes from Satan. In fact, the name Satan means "Accuser." Making the believer feel condemned is the devil's job, and he's very good at it. He knows that if he can make us feel condemned every time we falter, he can cause us to feel so hopeless and helpless that we'll never be able to live the victorious, fruitful life that Christ died to give us. Satan also wants to keep us feeling condemned because he knows it will make God seem distant from us, and this is one of his greatest deceptions. Yes, it should grieve our hearts when we sin, because sin grieves the heart of God. But the Lord doesn't want us wallowing in guilt and self-pity; He wants us to confess our sin, receive His forgiveness, ask for His help to overcome the sin, and then move on. The next time the devil tries to assail you with guilt and condemnation, remind him that you are the righteousness of God in Christ (2 Cor. 5:21), and the

greater One lives in you (1 John 4:4)—and claim the
victory that Jesus won for you! (1 Cor. 15:57.)

Take a Break

Memorize 1 John 1:9. Remind yourself when you have
thoughts of guilt and condemnation that God has forgiven you!

The High Cost of Unforgiveness

These verses illustrate what is perhaps the best reason for our being forgiving people. Jesus makes it clear that if we don't forgive others, we aren't forgiven by God. How we treat others is a major factor in determining the quality of our relationship with God. Even our prayer life is affected when our attitudes toward others are not right. In Mark chapter 11, when Jesus is teaching about mountain-moving faith, He concludes by saying that if we hold anything against anyone, we must forgive them. If we want our prayers to have power, we cannot hold grudges or harbor bitterness. In Matthew 5:23-24, Jesus tells us that before we offer a gift to God, if we have a grievance against anyone, we need to be reconciled with them. Then God will accept our gift.

> For if you forgive men when they sin against you, your heavenly Father will also forgive you. But if you do not forgive men their sins, your Father will not forgive your sins.
>
> Matthew 6:14,15

If you are holding a grudge against anyone right now, or if you are in strife with anyone, consider this. You could be opening a door for the enemy to come in and destroy your life, marriage, family, or friendships. In 2 Corinthians 2:10-11, Paul talks about forgiving the sinner after the church disciplines him. He says, "And what I have forgiven...I have forgiven in the sight of Christ for your sake, in order that Satan might not outwit us. For we are not unaware of his schemes." Paul reveals that by withholding forgiveness we can give the devil an advantage over us. I decided long ago that harboring resentment just isn't worth it. My relationship with God and my prayers are too valuable to me. Maybe you feel you have a right to withhold forgiveness from someone. But if you belong to the Lord, you gave up your rights when you became a member of His family. Colossians 3:13 says, "Bear with each other and forgive whatever grievances you may have against one another. Forgive as the Lord forgave you." How can we refuse to forgive others when God has so graciously forgiven us? Today, the Savior is reaching out to you and asking, "Won't you do it for Me?"

Prayer

Lord, forgive me for all the times I've harbored resentment toward others. Give me a heart like Yours so that I may be quick to forgive. When I'm tempted to hold anything against anyone, remind me how graciously You have forgiven me. Give me the grace and the wisdom to avoid conversations and situations that might lead to strife. Thank You that as I practice forgiveness, I will be blessed with a closer relationship with You!

The Power of Our Words

Death and life are in the power of the tongue, and they who indulge in it shall eat the fruit of it [for death or life].
Proverbs 18:21 AMP

The verses above, and many other Scriptures in the Bible, reveal that our words have tremendous power. We can speak life to ourselves and others, or we can speak death. If you need some convincing that this is true, look at what the Apostle Paul writes in Romans 10:9: "If you confess with your mouth, 'Jesus is Lord,' and believe in your heart that God raised him from the dead, you will be saved." Our words carry so much weight that they can even affirm our salvation and, therefore, affect the spiritual realm. Jesus warned us about taking our speech too lightly. In Matthew 12:36-37, He says, "But I tell you that men will have to give account on the day of judgment for every careless word they have spoken. For by your words you will be acquitted, and by your words you will be condemned."

It disturbs me to hear so many believers say things like, "The flu is going around, and I just know I'm going to get it. I always do!" Or, "My son drives like a maniac. It's just a matter of time before he kills himself or somebody else!" Or even, "My parents fight all the time. They're definitely going to get a divorce!" I believe with all my heart that this kind of talk grieves the heart of God. Hebrews 11:6 says that "without faith it is impossible to please God." What kind of faith are we demonstrating when we speak words of doom and destruction over our children or someone's marriage? Shouldn't we be praying and standing on God's promises for them instead? And when we say that we are certain to become victims of illness, aren't we putting more faith in that affliction than in God's ability and willingness to keep us well or heal us? Wouldn't we be much wiser—and wouldn't God be more pleased—if we prayed in faith for God's protection and healing? Knowing that our words can affect the spiritual realm, isn't it likely that when we're speaking words of sickness, destruction, and defeat, that we're opening doors for the Destroyer to come in and attack us and our loved ones? Our words are seeds, and it's up to us whether we plant seeds of life or death. If we want to reap the right kind of harvest, then we've got to plant the right kind of seeds.

Prayer

Lord, forgive me for the times my speech has been filled with doubt and destruction instead of faith and life. Cleanse my lips the way You did Isaiah's. (Isa. 6:6,7.) Help me to speak words that please You and bless others. Remind me of all Your precious promises of wholeness, life, and victory. Thank You that my words of life will bring people hope and healing!

Do You Want To Get Well?

Why is it that some people become bitter when they go through hard times, while others become better? Perhaps part of the answer lies in an old saying that still rings true today: "The same hot water that hardens an egg, softens a carrot." We don't always have a choice about what happens to us, but we do have the power to choose how we will respond to the difficulties that come our way.

> When Jesus saw him lying there and learned that he had been in this condition for a long time, He asked him, "Do you want to get well?"
>
> John 5:6

Jesus said, "If you do not forgive men their sins, your Father will not forgive your sins" (Matt. 6:15). Unforgiveness is serious business in God's eyes, and we need to view it the same way and act accordingly. Fortunately, we don't have to forgive others in our own strength. We have the Holy Spirit pouring the God-kind of love into our hearts as we walk with Him daily. (Rom. 5:5.) The Apostle Paul warns us that withholding forgiveness from others can open the door to satanic attack.

for Dads

(Eph. 4:26-28.) In at least two places in the Gospels, Jesus reveals a link between the effectiveness of our prayers and our obligation to forgive others. (Matt. 6:14,15; Mark 11:25.)

Perhaps the Lord is asking you today, "Do you want to get well?" No matter what you've been through or how many emotional scars you've built up over the years, healing and restoration are available to you. All you need to do is stop focusing on your wounds and begin focusing on the cure. There is no pain, injury, or hurt that the love of God cannot heal. I'm living proof of that, and so are many others. Ask the Lord to search your heart and reveal to you who it is you need to forgive. Then leave all your bitterness, resentment, and unforgiveness at the foot of the Cross—and let the healing begin!

Take a Break

Take a moment and ask God to bring healing to wounds you have from the past. The Holy Spirit will bring you comfort and restoration to the deepest part of you, no matter the offense.

Not Perfect? Read This!

Do you ever feel like you don't deserve God's gift of salvation? If you do, I know how you feel. These verses tell us that we don't have to earn salvation or God's love. We couldn't even if we wanted to. The truth is, we could never be "good enough" to save ourselves. That's exactly why God sent us a Savior. In fact, the Bible reveals that even our best efforts wouldn't measure up. Isaiah 64:6 says, "All our righteous acts are like filthy rags." But while we can't model perfection, we can model spiritual

It is clear, then, that God's promise to give the whole earth to Abraham and his descendants was not because Abraham obeyed God's laws but because he trusted God to keep his promise. So if you still claim that God's blessings go to those who are "good enough," then you are saying that God's promises to those who have faith are meaningless, and faith is foolish. But the fact of the matter is this: when we try to gain God's blessing and salvation by keeping his laws we always end up under his anger, for we always fail to keep them. The only way we can keep from breaking laws is not to have any to break! So God's blessings are given to us by faith, as a free gift.

Romans 4:13-16 TLB

for Dads

growth. Out of gratitude for God's gracious gift, we can seek to abide in Him and be fruitful for His glory. And we can serve Him and others out of a thankful heart.

Ephesians 2:8-9 says, "For it is by grace you have been saved, through faith—and this not from yourselves, it is the gift of God—not by works, so that no one can boast." One reason why God wants to make our salvation a gift is so that we can't boast about it or take the credit for it. God wants the glory, and He deserves it. Scripture reveals that when people asked Jesus, "What must we do to do the works God requires?" He answered them, "The work of God is this: to believe in the one he has sent" (John 6:28,29). We all know how much Jesus spoke about the importance of our doing good works and loving and serving God, but here He gives us the bottom line. It's not what we do that matters most to God; it's in whom we believe. It's not what we do that makes us righteous in God's sight; it's what He has done for us. Does that mean that the Bible condones sin? Not at all. Romans 6:2 says, "Shall we go on sinning so that grace may increase? By no means! We died to sin; how can we live in it any longer?" From the moment of salvation we are empowered by the Holy Spirit to resist sin and obey God. We become increasingly uncomfortable with sin, and God's ways become more attractive to us. And Scripture assures us that "God is at work within us, helping us want to obey him, and then helping us do what he wants" (Phil. 2:13 TLB).

Prayer

Lord, forgive me for trying to earn the salvation You want me to receive as a free gift. Help me to stop striving to please You and to learn to abide and rest in You. Give me a revelation of my new identity in Christ so that I can cooperate with Your plan for my spiritual growth. Thank You for showing me that it's not my perfection that counts, but Yours!

The Positive Power of Saying "No"

Since Jesus went through everything you're going through and more, learn to think like him. Think of your sufferings as a weaning from that old sinful habit of always expecting to get your own way. Then you'll be able to live out your days free to pursue what God wants instead of being tyrannized by what you want.

1 Peter 4:1,2
MESSAGE

The verses above were life-changing for me. They made me realize how doing what I feel like doing all the time allows my natural desires to bully me. The more I give in to myself, the harder it becomes to discipline myself to do the right thing. On the other hand, the more I resist my natural impulses to indulge myself, the more control and freedom I gain—which is what God wants for His children. For instance, often when I go shopping and get the impulse to buy something, I begin to feel a "tension" between my flesh and my spirit. My flesh may say, "You can't pass this up—it's on sale!" But my spirit will give me a "check" about it, warning me to resist the urge to buy it. Then I have to decide which I want to please more—my spirit or my flesh. Either way, I will have to endure some kind of suffering. If I say "no" to myself, my flesh will suffer. If I say "yes" to myself, my spirit will suffer. I've discovered that if I can't get out of a situation without suffering somehow, it's best if I suffer in my flesh, rather than in my spirit. That's the attitude Jesus had, and that's what the verses above are referring to. Every time we choose to suffer in our flesh rather than have our own way, sin's hold over us diminishes and it becomes easier to obey God. Before we accepted Christ as our Savior, there was no way we could have escaped the enslavement of sin. But with the gift of salvation comes the gift of the Holy Spirit, and the power to live a godly life in a fleshly body and a sinful world. God doesn't give us His Spirit just so we can live like the rest of the world. He gives us supernatural power so that we can say "no" to sin and live the abundant life that Jesus died to give us.

Take a Break

Where have you been saying "yes," when you should have been saying "no"? When you have the answer to that question, find Scriptures that strengthen your "no," and remain steadfast in their support.

Even Now

But I know that even now God will give you whatever you ask.

John 11:22

These words were spoken to Jesus by Martha, the sister of Lazarus. Her brother had already been dead four days by the time Jesus arrived. Yet here she confesses her faith in the Savior to do even the impossible. Moments later Martha witnesses a miracle as her brother is raised to life by the Master.

A few years ago God began bringing me up to a new level of faith. He taught me how to pray what I now refer to as my "even now" prayers. I would be facing an impossible situation, and it would seem like all the doors before me had been closed. My first impression would be to think, *I guess it just wasn't God's will.* Then I would sense another impression coming up in my spirit telling me to continue praying in faith. I might pray something like this: "Lord, I admit this looks like a hopeless situation, but I know that even now You can make a way where there seems to be none. I ask that You do that, Lord." I have seen so many seemingly closed doors opened by praying like this, that my prayer life has been radically changed forever. And I have used this principle in praying about small matters, as well as big ones.

Jesus said, "The things which are impossible with men are possible with God" (Luke 18:27 NKJV). I think it's sad that our society has gotten so sophisticated and cynical that we've forgotten how to pray for the impossible. In Jeremiah 32:27, the Lord says, "I am the Lord, the God of all mankind. Is anything too hard for me?" This statement should not only encourage us, but it should convict us as well. Psalm 77:19 TLB says, "Your road led by a pathway through the sea—a pathway no one knew was there!" The Israelites never could have imagined that God would make a way for them through the Red Sea. Likewise, when we pray for the impossible, God will often make a way for us that will exceed our expectations. Psalm 77:14 TLB says, "You are the God of miracles and wonders! You still demonstrate your awesome power." When we ask God for the impossible, we invite Him to work wonders in our lives—something He delights in doing.

Take a Break

Have you given up on a dream or vision that God has planted in your heart, because at this point it looks like it can never come to pass? What "impossible" situations do you have in your life right now that maybe you've given up on too soon? Write down exactly what you are believing God to do and today's date next to it. Commit it to God. Hang on to what you have written. You will be able to look back and have a documented record of His extraordinary faithfulness.

Ignoring Words of Doubt

In the above verses, Jairus had appealed to Jesus to come and heal his daughter, who was seriously ill. Before they arrived at Jairus's house, they were told that the little girl had already died. Scripture reveals that the Master ignored their comments and asked Jairus to "just trust Him." Each time we're in a trial, we're going to have to choose between trusting God and believing the "negative reports" of others. During difficult times we can be very vulnerable to the remarks that people make about our circumstances, and if

> "…Messengers arrived from Jairus's home with the message, 'Your daughter's dead. There's no use in troubling the Teacher now.' But Jesus ignored their comments and said to Jairus, 'Don't be afraid. Just trust me.'"
>
> Mark 5:35,36 NLT

we're not careful, we'll take their negative words to heart and become fearful and depressed. If the people around us are not led by God's Spirit, we're not likely to hear God's view of our situation from them. They'll usually give us the world's view, and you can bet it will be one of doom and gloom, especially if it's a particularly serious or "hopeless" situation. They haven't gotten a revelation of how powerful and loving our God is, and how He delights in working wonders for His children who put their faith in Him. And we shouldn't be too surprised if sometimes even fellow believers don't see our situation through God's eyes. Often the Lord will reveal only to us that He has a plan for our deliverance. That's why it's so important for us to ignore others when they make comments filled with doubt and unbelief. We need to turn to God and ask Him to give us His view of our situation. Sometimes all we'll hear from Him is "Just trust Me." Sometimes that's all we'll need.

If you're in a trial today, let this promise from God encourage your heart: "Trust Me in your times of trouble, and I will rescue you, and you will give Me glory"! (Ps. 50:15 NLT).

Prayer

Lord, help me to ignore the negative comments of others whenever I go through difficult times. Teach me to listen for Your words of encouragement and hope. Give me the faith to trust You for my deliverance, and guard me from fear and doubt. Thank You for the wonders You'll work in my life as I trust in You!

Overlooked and Unappreciated

Whatever you do, work at it with all your heart, as working for the Lord, not for men, since you know that you will receive an inheritance from the Lord as a reward. It is the Lord Christ you are serving.

Colossians 3:23,24 NLT

Sooner or later all of us will experience the pain and disappointment of having our efforts ignored, minimized, or criticized by others. I believe that how we respond in times like these not only indicates our level of spiritual maturity, but also determines our outcome. One thing that helps me is remembering that whatever we do should be done "unto the Lord." The verses above clearly convey the perspective we should have in all we do. If we focus on pleasing God and doing our best in everything, we won't be so resentful, hurt, or discouraged when others don't appreciate or reward our efforts. Instead, we can rest secure in the knowledge that God is fully aware of all we do, and He will see that we get the recognition and reward we deserve in His perfect way and timing. Even if those we are working for are continually unreasonable or unfair, we can take heart from God's reassurance that "nothing can hinder the Lord" (1 Sam. 14:6 NLT). There may be times when it looks like others are succeeding in delaying or preventing our progress, but the truth is that when God decides to bless and promote His people, no person on earth and no devil in hell can stop Him. If you can relate to this message today, let me encourage you to get your eyes off other people and get them squarely on God. Work hard and do your best in all you do, trusting that the Lord Himself will honor you for it, even if others don't. Let your declaration of faith be the Psalmist's—"You will give me greater honor than before, and turn again and comfort me"! (Ps. 71:21 TLB).

Take a Break

When you're tempted to feel overlooked and unappreciated, encourage yourself with the Scriptures above. Read them, meditate upon them, and be enlivened by them!

A Prophet Without Honor

Then Jesus told them, "A prophet is honored everywhere except in his own hometown and among his relatives and his own family."

Mark 6:4 NLT

The Bible reveals that some of Jesus' friends and family were not the least bit impressed with His ministry or His accomplishments. In fact, the Bible says that His own family thought He was "out of his mind" (Mark 3:21). Jesus was misunderstood because of His devotion to the Father and His dedication to the work His Father assigned Him. Why should we be surprised when our loved ones don't understand our commitment to God? The Apostle Paul was often misunderstood, too. In 2 Corinthians 5:13, he says, "If we are out of our mind, it is for the sake of God." Seems to me that if people think we have lost our minds because of our love for God, we're in good company.

The truth is that when we decide to live for God, people are not always going to understand or respect us for it. Paul explains why: "The man without the Spirit does not accept the things that come from the Spirit of God, for they are foolishness to him, and he cannot understand them, because they are spiritually discerned" (1 Cor. 2:14). Now that we have the Holy Spirit living in us, we are able to see things from God's perspective. The way we view things will often be radically different than the way others do, and because of that, our priorities will be different. Have you ever accomplished something wonderful for God, and then been met with indifference and disinterest from your friends and loved ones? I have. It can turn our joy into hurt and frustration pretty quickly. Some time ago I gained some media attention because of my work for the Lord. Some of my friends and family were not the least bit impressed. What bothered me most was knowing that if I had been in the public eye because of a sports-related achievement, or because I wrote romance novels, they would have been thrilled. But because I was being recognized for my service to God, they held no esteem for my accomplishments. That was a painful realization for me. Since then I've decided to serve the Lord with all my heart, even if no one else cares. Paul's words in Philippians 3:13-14 have been a great inspiration to me: "But one thing I do: forgetting what lies behind and reaching forward to what lies ahead, I press on toward the goal for the prize of the upward call of God in Christ Jesus." I'm going on with God. How about you?

Prayer

Lord, thank You for the opportunities You've given me to serve You. Help me to remember that when others don't respect or honor my service to You, it doesn't diminish its value or usefulness in Your sight. Today I renew my wholehearted commitment to You, and I ask You to use me in new and exciting ways for Your glory!

Favor With God and Man

For most of my life I had repeatedly heard the verses in the Bible that talked about how those who were devoted to the Lord would suffer persecution and criticism from others. I got the impression that I always had to choose between having God's favor or man's. Once I started delving into the Scriptures, I realized that many times I could enjoy both. The verse above promises us favor in the sight of God and man when we walk in God's ways. The Apostle Paul records a similar statement in Romans 14:18, where he describes true kingdom behavior and says, "Anyone who serves Christ in this way is pleasing to God and approved by men." The truth is that if we just concentrate on pleasing God, He will give us favor with others when we need it most. We can even ask God to give us favor with others. When we do that, we're not being selfish or prideful, but scriptural.

> Let love and faithfulness never leave you; bind them around your neck, write them on the tablet of your heart. Then you will win favor and a good name in the sight of God and man.
>
> Proverbs 3:4

It's true that believers who are really committed to God will sometimes experience criticism and persecution. Jesus said we could count on it. He wanted us to know what we were getting into when we made the decision to follow Him. If we're making a difference for God, we can't expect Satan to just sit back and do nothing to try to hinder us. But the Bible teaches us that we can pray for God's favor, which can be a powerful weapon against the enemy's attacks. Psalm 89:17 NLT says, "Our power is based on Your favor." And Psalm 5:12 says, "Surely, O Lord, You bless the righteous; You surround them with Your favor as with a shield." We are God's children, His chosen, His elect. And He is committed to protecting and providing for His own. When we concentrate on pleasing God, we can depend on Him to change people's hearts for our benefit. Proverbs 16:7 says, "When a man's ways are pleasing to the Lord, He makes even his enemies live at peace with him." If God is willing and able to change the hearts of our enemies, surely we can expect Him to give us favor in the sight of our teachers, employers, neighbors, and others we come in contact with. But we mustn't assume that this favor is automatic. Often we will have to ask God for it, expecting Him to act on our behalf. When you pray for favor, people will bless you and they won't even know why. Begin today to pray for favor, and discover for yourself that "the Lord bestows favor and honor" upon His people! (Ps. 84:11).

Take a Break

Start every morning this week with a declaration of favor over your life. When you wake up, say aloud, "I have the favor of God over my life. I have favor with both God and man. Everywhere I go and everything I touch is blessed!"

God-Pleasers Vs. Man-Pleasers

Am I now trying to win the approval of men, or of God? Or am I trying to please men? If I were still trying to please men, I would not be a servant of Christ.
Galatians 1:10

This verse warns us that if we are to be true servants of God, we must seek the Lord's approval, rather than man's. Very often God's will and man's are opposed to each other, and here's where the tension arises. Jesus said, "What is highly valued among men is detestable in God's sight" (Luke 16:15). God and man have very different value systems, and we are expected to make right choices, even in tough situations. In Luke 12:48, Jesus tells us, "From everyone who has been given much, much will be demanded; and from the one who has been entrusted with much, much more will be asked." As children of God, we are equipped with the power of the Holy Spirit to live by God's standards, not the world's. The Bible assures us that our God is a just God, and He will never give us unattainable goals to strive for. When we supply the will, He supplies the power. Exodus 23:2 says, "Do not follow the crowd in doing wrong." Jesus said, "Unless you are faithful in small matters, you won't be faithful in large ones" (Luke 16:10 NLT). Don't be deceived into thinking that God doesn't care about the little details of our daily lives. He cares very much, and He expects us to be faithful. Proverbs 25:26 says, "If the godly compromise with the wicked, it is like polluting a fountain or muddying a spring." Not only can our compromise harm our fellowship with God, but it can damage our witness and cost us an opportunity to lead others to the Lord. It's been said that, "People may doubt what you say, but they will believe what you do." Instead of just telling them about Jesus, we need to show them Jesus! We're always appalled when we hear the biblical account of Peter denying Jesus. But look what the Apostle Paul says in Titus 1:16: "They claim to know God, but by their actions they deny him." We're no better than Peter when we choose to live our own way, rather than God's. The Bible says that "friendship with the world is hatred toward God" (James 4:4). God's not going to settle for a superficial commitment from us. We have a higher calling on our lives, and it's the Lord's desire to use us for His glory. But He can't use us if we won't submit to His ways and plans for us. In 1 Timothy 1:12, Paul says, "I thank Christ Jesus our Lord, who has given me strength, that he considered me faithful, appointing me to his service." God has promised to reward our faithfulness by giving us opportunities to serve Him. But there are other rewards for choosing to please God rather than people. When we make it our life's goal to please the Lord, the result is joy, peace, and fulfillment. On the other hand, whenever we try to please other people, we experience frustration, disappointment, and emptiness. The truth is that living to please God is the only decent way to live.

Prayer

Lord, forgive me for the times I chose to please other people instead of You. Give me the strength and courage I need to resist the temptation to win the approval of others. Help me to be faithful in little things so that You can trust me to be faithful in bigger ones. Thank You for rewarding my faithfulness with wonderful opportunities to serve You!

Rejoicing in Our Labor

The Bible makes it abundantly clear that God wants us to enjoy our work. Solomon puts it plainly when he says, "To enjoy your work...that is indeed a gift from God" (Eccl. 5:19 NLT). This is a common theme throughout the

> To enjoy your work and accept your lot in life— that is indeed a gift from God.
> Ecclesiastes 5:19 NLT

Book of Ecclesiastes. Solomon also writes, "That everyone may eat and drink, and find satisfaction in all his toil—this is the gift of God" (Eccl. 3:13). So now that we know that God wants us to find joy and satisfaction in our work— and that these are gifts from Him—what can we do? We can ask Him for them, trusting that He is true to His Word when He says that whenever we pray in line with His will, He will answer us. (1 John 5:14,15.) Jesus said, "If you, then, though you are evil, know how to give good gifts to your children, how much more will your Father in heaven give good gifts to those who ask him!" (Matt. 7:11). And James wrote, "You do not have, because you do not ask God" (James 4:2). The key word in these verses is *ask*. Don't assume that you have to settle for doing distasteful and unfulfilling work all your life. Yes, there may be times when we might have to endure some periods of doing work we dislike, but our prayer and our goal should be to spend most of our lives doing the kind of work that gives us joy. One of my regular prayers for myself and my family is, "Lord, please enable us to earn a good living doing what we love to do most." I also pray that God will help us to do our part in the fulfillment of this prayer. One way we can cooperate with the Lord to this end is to seek His guidance daily, depending on Him to keep us in His perfect will. When we're doing what God has called us to do, we will experience a peace, joy, and satisfaction that will be missing when we're out of His will.

I encourage you to begin asking God to make a way for you to enjoy your work. If you're in a position where you really dislike your job or the work you're doing, the Lord can open up a new door of opportunity for you as a result of your prayers. If it's not His will and timing for you to make a move right now, He can make your present job more pleasant and fulfilling somehow. He may do that by causing you to find favor or recognition in the sight of your employer or coworkers. Or, He may improve your working conditions in various little ways until He can move you into a more desirable position. But rest assured that as you pray in faith, God will do something to enable you to enjoy your labor more.

Take a Break

Enjoying your work is, indeed, a gift from God. So, graciously accept the Lord's gift and begin thanking Him for the reality of it to come to pass in your life!

Forget the Results

> "Master, we've worked hard all night and haven't caught anything. But because you say so, I will let down the nets."
> Luke 5:5

I can really relate to poor Peter here when, after fishing all night and catching nothing, the Lord asks him to let down his net one more time. It's as if Peter is saying, "Lord, I've worked hard and long, but I have nothing to show for it!" The only thing that motivates Peter to drop that net again is the Lord's command. As a result of his obedience, Peter is rewarded with a catch of fish that begins to break his nets and sink two boats. The disciple could have let his weariness and discouragement rob him of a miracle, but fortunately, he put his feelings aside and obeyed the Lord.

Our society has become so result-oriented. Too often we're initially excited about a new assignment that the Lord gives us, but as soon as we realize we aren't getting the results we expected, we quit and give up. I experienced this for myself when my son started a Bible club in his public high school. After the initial excitement began to wear off, my son and I were tempted to "throw in the towel." We were working long and hard, and instead of the club growing in number, it was diminishing. It seemed like resistance was coming against us from all directions—including from some of the school authorities, teachers, and students. We wrestled with that quitter's attitude that says, "Who needs this?!" Then the Lord spoke to our hearts. He told us not to worry about the results or the numbers. He told us to just be there for the kids that showed up, even if it was just a handful. And He told us to pray. If only two people came, they could pray and expect Jesus to be in their midst, like He promised. We stuck it out and didn't let our discouragement talk us out of doing God's will—and it paid off big time. The club grew, and over a period of five years it touched and changed the lives of hundreds of kids. The fact is that when God gives us a job to do, even if it's just to pray or witness to someone, He doesn't want us focusing on the results. There will be times when it seems like we have nothing to show for our hard work. But if we obey God and keep going, the day will come when we'll be rewarded with a net-breaking, boat-sinking catch of our own. Be encouraged by this promise from God: "Let us not get tired of doing what is right, for after a while we will reap a harvest of blessing if we don't get discouraged and give up"! (Gal. 6:9 TLB).

Prayer

Lord, when You give me a job to do, help me not to focus on the results. Help me, instead, to focus on You and Your will. When it seems like I have nothing to show for my work, send me the encouragement I need to keep going. As I'm faithful, use me to touch and change more and more lives. Thank You for the harvest of blessings I'll reap!

Four Steps to Success

Several years ago I heard a godly man offer some advice about how we can enjoy more of the peace and joy that the Lord wants us to have, even in the midst of trouble and uncertainty. He said that if we will make the following statements our personal declarations, and if we will practice the principles behind them, we will gain the victory in every trial we encounter. If we look at each statement in the light of Scripture, we can see that they are all based on sound biblical principles.

1. "I'm not going to worry about that." Philippians 4:6-7 NLT says, "Don't worry about anything; instead, pray about everything. Tell God what you need, and thank Him for all He has done. If you do this, you will experience God's peace, which is far more wonderful than the human mind can understand. His peace will guard your hearts and minds as you live in Christ Jesus." Anxiety and worry are rooted in fear, and fear will hinder our faith and trust in God. If you're worrying about something, perhaps you need to pray about it more. Keeping it before God in prayer will help you

focus more on Him and His abilities, and less on your-self and your inabilities.

2. "I'm not going to try to figure that out." One of the hardest things I've had to learn as a true believer in Christ is that I must no longer try to solve my prob-lems my own way. Instead, I must turn to my divine Problem Solver and depend on Him to show me the way. He tells us, "My thoughts are not your thoughts, neither are your ways My ways. As the heavens are higher than the earth, so are My ways higher than your ways and My thoughts than your thoughts" (Isa. 55:8,9). Our thinking is severely limited, while God's is not. Even when we can't find a single solution to our problem, God has more than a million ways to solve it. But He may not reveal the answer until we stop wrestling with the matter and leave it in His hands.

3. "I'm not going to try to make something happen." When we're in a trial and it seems like God isn't moving fast enough to suit us, it can be tempting to try to "kick down doors." But we'd be wise to remem-ber that getting ahead of God and trying to make our own way can not only delay our blessings, but keep us from receiving God's best. The fact is that we are more likely to make mistakes when we fail to wait on

God, than when we fail to move on His cue. Isaiah wrote, "The Lord is a faithful God. Blessed are those who wait for Him to help them" (Isa. 30:18 NLT).

4. "I'm going to trust God!" Heeding this single foundational biblical principle will help us avoid all of the obstacles that the previous three statements are designed to overcome. If we're trusting God, we're much less likely to worry, to try to figure things out for ourselves, or to try to make something happen on our own. Scripture says, "Trust in the Lord with all your heart; do not depend on your own understanding. Seek His will in all you do, and He will direct your paths" (Prov. 3:5,6 NLT). If we will turn to God and seek His perfect will for us in every situation—laying aside our own preconceived notions and solutions—we can depend on Him to lead us in the paths of His very best blessings.

Take a Break

Begin to declare these statements over your life. When you do this, you are guaranteed success!

Prepare for Promotion

Do not despise this small beginning, for the eyes of the Lord rejoice to see the work begin....
Zechariah 4:10 TLB

Sometimes God assigns us small tasks which can seem insignificant to us. But in God's sight, there are no unimportant tasks in His kingdom. Sometimes the Lord expects us to prove our faithfulness in little matters before He gives us larger assignments. In Matthew 25:24, Jesus says, "You have been faithful with a few things; I will put you in charge of many things." The Lord is teaching us here that if we will be faithful in the duties He assigns us, promotion will be our reward. At times we can become tempted to promote ourselves, but God's Word makes it clear that job belongs to the Lord. "For promotion and power come from nowhere on earth, but only from God. He promotes one and deposes another" (Ps. 75:6,7 TLB). Perhaps God has given you work to do and you feel as though it has little value or that it's having little impact. Maybe you're receiving very little thanks or recognition. Or you're being met with more resistance than cooperation. Perhaps a previous task the Lord had given you was more appealing than the one you're involved with now. But God doesn't take pleasure in our work for Him only if it's big and important. He rejoices when we do the job He's given us, no matter what the size or significance. If you'll faithfully do the work the Lord's called you to do right now, He will promote you when it will benefit you most. Take heart, for today God's promise to you is—"Humble yourselves, therefore, under God's mighty hand, that he may lift you up in due time"! (1 Peter 5:6).

Prayer

Lord, forgive me when I feel dissatisfied with the work You've given me to do. Cause me to realize that there are no insignificant tasks in Your kingdom. When I'm tempted to try to promote myself instead of waiting on You, remind me that my efforts will be fruitless in the end. Help me to recognize the jobs You've committed to me and to carry them out faithfully. Thank You that at the proper time You will reward me with promotion!

Don't Get Lazy

> Don't drag your feet. Be like those who stay the course with committed faith and then get everything promised to them.
>
> Hebrews 6:12
> MESSAGE

Recently, some of the problems my family and I had experienced in our neighborhood in the past arose once again. When they first resurfaced, I felt somewhat confused and bewildered. I had prayed and stood on God's promises for peace for my "borders" (Ps. 147:14), and I had witnessed the delivering power of God in mighty ways. But I had begun to take God's blessings for granted. When the problems threatened once again, I sought the Lord for the reason. He promptly pointed out to me that my prayers in that area had gone from earnest to anemic. And He reminded me that I needed to continue to stand in faith for the peace of my neighborhood if I wanted to regain and maintain the victory I had won before.

Hebrews 6:12 says, "We do not want you to become lazy, but to imitate those who through faith and patience inherit what has been promised." I realized that I had become a "spiritual sluggard"—as the Amplified version of this verse says—at least where this issue was concerned. When the problem was at its worst, I used my faith and patience to lay hold of God's promises for the situation. But as soon as the problem showed signs of subsiding, I slacked off. That was a big mistake. Even so, it was a reminder of how important it is for us to continue to stand in faith for God's blessings, even when it looks like our prayers have already been answered. Proverbs 13:4 says, "The sluggard craves and gets nothing, but the desires of the diligent are fully satisfied." Those of us who want God's blessings badly enough to diligently pray for them will find that diligence produces results. Do you ever feel like you want to take a "spiritual vacation"? I do. But I have found that spiritual passivity can be very costly. Are there areas in your life in which you've spiritually "slacked off"? If so, you may be hindering the flow of God's blessings into your life. Don't make the devil's job easy for him. Satan is relentless, and we need to be relentless, too. Talk to the Lord about any areas in your life that you might be neglecting spiritually, and ask Him to help you get back on track. It won't be long before you're reaping a harvest of blessings that keeps on coming!

Take a Break

Don't make the devil's job easy today! Instead, ask yourself if there are areas in your life in which you've spiritually "slacked off." Armed with that information, stand on the promises of God and pray with new vigor.

God's Perfect Timing

There are times when it appears that God is saying "no" to us, but He's actually saying "wait." The Bible often uses phrases like "the appointed time" or "the proper time." Solomon wrote, "There is a proper time and procedure for every matter" (Eccl. 8:6). Ours is not a "hit-or-miss" God. He created us with specific plans and purposes in mind, and His timing is always perfect. Scripture says, "But these things I plan won't happen right away. Slowly, steadily, surely, the time approaches when the vision will be fulfilled. If it seems slow, do not despair, for these things will surely come to pass. Just be patient! They will not be overdue a single day!" (Hab. 2:3 TLB). As long as our trust is in God and we are praying and seeking Him daily, we can be sure that He is busy working behind the scenes to bring our God-given dreams and visions to pass. The Lord instructs us to be

> For the vision is yet for an appointed time and it hastens to the end [fulfillment]; it will not deceive or disappoint. Though it tarry, wait [earnestly] for it, because it will surely come; it will not be behindhand on its appointed day.
>
> Habakkuk 2:3 AMP

patient and not to despair, because He knows that impatience and discouragement can cause us to miss out on His best for us. Sometimes God makes us wait because certain circumstances are not yet right for us. Other times we're the ones who are not yet ready, or someone else involved is not prepared. As long as we are praying and believing God to work all things out for our good (Rom. 8:28), we can trust that He is actively working in our circumstances, in our lives, and in the lives of others. If you are waiting on God for some special blessing or breakthrough today, remember that delays are not necessarily denials. Keep your faith and hope in God, believing that at just the right time He will open doors for you. When He does, you will know without a doubt that it was worth the wait!

Take a Break

Are you consumed with the future? Find three things about the present that you will miss once they have passed. It may be your toddler's crawling stage or precious moments with your aging parents. Whatever the present holds, savor it. The future will arrive soon enough in God's perfect timing.

From Trials to Triumphs

Paul and Silas were thrown into prison in Philippi for casting a demon out of a young slave girl who had been earning her master a lot of money. The disciples were stripped, beaten, and chained in a cell. The next thing that happened still amazes me, no matter how often I read it in Scripture. Paul and Silas began to pray and praise God in song. Most of us would have been grumbling and drowning in self-pity. We might have said something like, "God, here I am trying to serve You and lead others to You. How could You let these people do this to me? I don't deserve this!" Fortunately, instead of complaining, these disciples praised God, who responded by miraculously setting His servants free from captivity. As a result, the jailer and his entire household became believers.

> About midnight Paul and Silas were praying and singing hymns to God, and the other prisoners were listening to them. Suddenly there was such a violent earthquake that the foundations of the prison were shaken. At once all the prison doors flew open, and everybody's chains came loose.
>
> Acts 16:25,26

Perhaps you are in a trial of your own today. Maybe the last thing you feel like doing is praising God. But listen to what Scripture teaches us. David said in Psalm 34:1, "I will bless the Lord at all times; his praise shall continually be in my mouth." And he meant it. Whether David was experiencing good times or bad, he praised God. Just one example of this is in 2 Samuel 12:20, where David and Bathsheba's infant son has just died as part of God's chastisement of the couple. The first thing David does is "go into the house of the Lord and worship God." This is just one of the many reasons why God called David a man after His own heart. And though the Lord allowed His servant to suffer the consequences of his sins, He gave David victory over all his enemies and blessed him with great wealth and honor. Paul and Silas praised God in the darkest of circumstances and unbelievers turned to Christ. If you'll praise God in your trials, your example could very well attract the attention of those who won't be reached any other way. Not only that, but you may find that the Lord will turn your trials into triumphs!

Take a Break

Whether you're experiencing an "up" or a "down"—and even if it's midnight in your circumstances—stop right now and offer up thanksgiving, praise, and worship to the Lord!

Pursue Perseverance

Pursue righteousness, godliness, faith, love, perseverance and gentleness.

1 Timothy 6:11
NASB

The dictionary defines *persevere* as "To continue in some effort, course of action, in spite of difficulty, opposition; be steadfast in purpose."[1] I like to think of it as a "holy determination," born of the Holy Spirit. The Bible talks a lot about perseverance, because without it we could never fulfill our God-given purpose. In Luke 8:15, in the parable of the seed sower, Jesus says, "But the seed on good soil stands for those with a noble and good heart, who hear the Word, retain it, and by persevering produce a crop." Perseverance will enable us to be fruitful for God. It will aid us in holding on to God's promises and obeying His Word when times get tough and we're tempted to lose heart. Hebrews says, "You need to persevere so that when you have done the will of God, you will receive what he has promised" (Heb. 10:36). Scripture says that if we want to be effective witnesses for Christ, we need to "watch our lives and doctrine closely" and "persevere in them" (1 Tim. 4:16). Let's face it—lukewarm Christianity isn't going to do much to change the world. Unbelievers don't want to just hear about Jesus; they want to see Jesus in us, and that calls for a holy determination. And what about prayer? Luke 18:1 says, "One day, Jesus told his disciples a story to illustrate their need for constant prayer, and to show them that they must never give up." When we are persistent in prayer, we can literally wear the devil out and stop him in his tracks. Each time we resist temptation and walk in obedience instead of giving up or giving in, we strengthen our resolve to do God's will and to walk in the victory that Jesus bought for us on Calvary. In Revelation 2:3, Jesus commends His people's steadfastness: "You have perse-vered and have endured hardships for My name, and have not grown weary." Jesus never said it would be easy—He just said it would be worth it! When weariness threatens to overwhelm us in trying times, we can call on our God "who gives perseverance and encouragement" to give us the grace to endure, and eventually triumph (Rom. 15:5 NASB). James 5:11 MESSAGE talks about the blessings Job reaped as a result of his perseverance. "What a gift life is to those who stay the course! You've heard, of course, of Job's staying power, and you know how God brought it all together for him at the end. That's because God cares, cares right down to the last detail"!

Prayer

Lord, give me the perseverance I need to do Your will so that I can receive the fulfillment of Your promises. Enable me to "run with perseverance the race marked out for me" (Heb. 12:1). When weariness threatens to overwhelm me, strengthen and refresh me, according to Your Word. (Ps. 68:9; Isa. 40:29.) Thank You that as I refuse to give up, I'll reap a harvest of blessings!

Good Things Vs. God Things

Maybe you've heard the saying, "Not every 'good' thing is a 'God' thing." In other words, there's no guarantee that everything "good" that we get involved with is God's will for us. In fact, one of Satan's most effective ploys is to try to get us sidetracked doing "good" things

> Teach me to do Your will, for You are my God; may Your good Spirit lead me on level ground.
> Psalm 143:10

so that we won't be able to fulfill our God-given purpose. That's why it's so important for us to seek God each day through prayer and Bible study, maintaining an attitude that says, "God, what is Your will for me as far as this is concerned?" If we don't, we'll keep getting involved with things that God never meant for us to simply because someone talked us into them, or because we think we "should." What usually happens then is that we end up hating our involvement, and we get little value or satisfaction out of it. Besides that, our efforts will most likely drain us, instead of lift us up and edify us. And because we don't have a "right heart" about the whole thing, we can't expect God to reward us for it, even though it may be benefiting others. God doesn't want us being led by our past experiences, but by His Spirit. He also doesn't want us being led by other people. It's only when we are where God wants us to be that we experience the fullness of His blessings. In the Psalms, David prayed, "Teach me to do Your will, for You are my God; may Your good Spirit lead me on level ground" (Ps. 143:10). While we should always have an attitude that seeks to do good, our main focus should not be on doing good things, but on doing God's will for us. Maintaining an attitude like this will take a lot of pressure off of us and enable us to walk in the freedom that God wants us to enjoy.

The next time you're faced with an opportunity to do something good, don't just assume that it's God's will for you. Instead, pause long enough to ask for His wisdom and guidance in the matter, making certain that it's not just good—but God!

Prayer

Lord, teach me how to avoid getting involved with things that are not Your best for me. Show me how to seek You continually and to be led by Your Spirit. Thank You, Lord, that as I follow You daily, my life will be fulfilling and fruitful!

Keeping Our Dreams in Proper Perspective

Each one should use whatever gift he has received to serve others, faithfully administering God's grace in its various forms. If anyone serves, he should do it with the strength God provides, so that in all things God may be praised through Jesus Christ.

1 Peter 4:10,11

There's nothing wrong with having visions, dreams, and goals. God wants us to have these things. But He wants us to have goals that line up with His will for us. When we get into agreement with God's will and purposes for our lives, there's no devil in hell, no person on earth, that can stop them from coming to pass. In fact, the only one who can really stand between us and our God-given destiny is us. Satan can't. Our families can't. Our bosses can't. Even the government can't. No one can prevent us from becoming the person of God that we were created to be. Except us. We can live our lives the way we want to, and we can turn our backs on God's perfect plans for us, if we so choose. And in the end, all we will have to show for it is regret. Or we can get in line with God's will for us, and we can watch Him unfold our lives like a beautiful flower, one petal at a time. We can do this by surrendering ourselves to the Lord—spirit, soul, and body—and by seeking Him and His will for us every day of our lives through prayer, devotion, and the study of His Word.

One thing I've learned is this: God will test our devotion to Him by letting us experience times of disappointment, especially where the fulfillment of our dreams is concerned. How we respond to these disappointments will help determine how much God can use us and bless us. If we respond with pouting, sulking, complaining, or threatening, God will have to treat us like the babies we're imitating, and He will not be able to trust us with the level of responsibility or blessing He longs to. But if we respond with an attitude that says—"God, I don't understand this, and it really hurts, but I believe that You are good, and You will work this out for my good"—the Lord will reward our faithfulness and spiritual maturity beyond our highest expectations.

If God has closed a door on a heartfelt desire or dream of yours today, take comfort in the fact that He is saying to you one of two things. Either it's, "Wait. It's not the right time yet." Or, "I have something better for you." In either case, you can't lose, because you have put your trust in a God who loves you with a perfect love and who has your best interests at heart!

Take a Break

Refocus your dreams. Take five minutes and write down what you would like to accomplish in the future. Pray and commit these desires to God in light of His will for your life.

Fulfilling Our God-Given Purpose

Since my son John was a young teenager, he earnestly wanted to make a difference for God. The Lord led him to start a Christian Web site, Jesusfreakhideout.com, when he was only 16 years old, and it has steadily grown and reached more and more people each year. Even so, he has wrestled with feelings of discourage-

> For we are God's workmanship, created in Christ Jesus to do good works, which God prepared in advance for us to do.
> Ephesians 2:10

ment and frustration from time to time. When he shares these feelings with me, I do my best to encourage him and to help him persevere. On one of these occasions recently, he was pouring out his heart to me and asking questions like—"How can I make a real difference when the grand scheme of things is so big? Is all of my seemingly endless work worth it? Does it have a point? Aren't there plenty of other people doing the same thing—and better? If they're getting more rewards than I am, does that mean I'm not on the right track? Sometimes I feel like I'm going against the wind—uphill!"

I've often wrestled with many of these same feelings and questions, and I was painfully aware of what he was going through. After all, what am I doing for God that millions of other people aren't? Not only are countless people doing the same thing that I am, but many of them are doing it better, and achieving bigger and better results. On days when I let these things get me down, I try to remind myself of some uplifting truths that the Lord has taught me over the years. One of them is that I have been created by God with a very specific purpose in mind, and that He has prepared good works for me that only I can do. The Bible says, "For we are God's workmanship, created in Christ Jesus to do good works, which God prepared in advance for us to do" (Eph. 2:10). The Lord has prepared for me achievements that only I can accomplish in this life. Even the most gifted person in the world cannot accomplish my personal God-given assignments. It's entirely possible that there are lost people on this earth who will only be reached by me, as I carry out my God-given purpose and destiny. That fact alone is usually enough to keep me going when I'm tempted to quit and give up.

I've discovered that it's easy for me to lose my focus if I concentrate too much on what other people are doing. But if I stay focused on fulfilling the call of God on my own life, I can persevere in the toughest of times. I remind myself that God didn't create me to copy or imitate anyone else. He created me to fulfill my own unique, God-given purpose and potential. And I can only do that by earnestly seeking His will for my life—by living each day in total dependence upon Him, and being sensitive and obedient to His Spirit's leading in all things. Scripture says, "The Lord will fulfill His purpose for me" (Ps. 138:8). As I concentrate on living for God and doing His will, I can count on Him to guide my steps in the paths that He has marked out for me. And I know that it's only in these paths that I will find the peace, joy, fulfillment, and success that are mine in Christ.

If it's your heart's desire to become all that God created you to be and to accomplish all the things He prepared for you in advance, please know that He will equip you with everything you need to succeed. I can't promise that you won't experience times of doubt or discouragement. But I can promise that if you'll keep your eyes on God and follow His lead, He will move mountains to make sure that His highest purposes for your life prevail!

Prayer

Lord, today I offer You all that I am and all that I have. I ask You to equip me with everything I need to fulfill my God-given purpose and potential. Help me not to focus on what others are doing, but to focus on You and Your call on my life. Send me special encouragement when I get discouraged or doubtful. Thank You that as I continually seek to follow Your will for my life, I will enjoy divine favor, victory, and success!

Grace Under Pressure

Jesus makes it clear in these verses that He expects a lot from us, especially in the area of how we relate to others. Though it may be "natural" for us to respond to mistreatment with anger or hostility, we are called to live "supernatural" lives through the grace and power of the Holy Spirit living in us. Jesus is not impressed when we are good to those who are good to us, because even unbelievers are capable of doing that. But He expects us to do the right thing, even when the right thing is not being done to us. Jesus knew what it was like to be mistreated. He was kind, compassionate, and good, yet He was still persecuted wherever He went. And He warned His disciples that they could expect the same treatment. In John

> ...Love your enemies, do good to those who hate you, bless those who curse you, pray for those who mistreat you.... Do to others as you would have them do to you.... If you love those who love you, what credit is that to you? Even 'sinners' love those who love them. And if you do good to those who are good to you, what credit is that to you? Even 'sinners' do that.
>
> Luke 6:27-28,31-33

15:18 and 20, Jesus tells us, "If the world hates you, keep in mind that it hated me first.... No servant is greater than his master. If they persecuted me, they will persecute you also." Knowing this, we have to decide if we are going to live our lives reacting like everyone else in these situations, or responding the way Jesus expects us to.

Romans chapter 12, Paul teaches us how to respond to those who mistreat us. "Do not repay anyone evil for evil.... Do not take revenge, my friends, but leave room for God's wrath, for it is written: 'It is mine to avenge; I will repay,' says the Lord.... Do not be overcome by evil, but overcome evil with good" (vv. 17,19,21). It's God's job to judge others, not ours. If we take matters into our own hands, we don't "leave room for God's wrath," and God may not intervene in the situation at all because we haven't given Him place. He may feel that our retaliation is punishment enough for the one who wronged us. But if we leave the matter in God's hands, though we are letting the person off the hook, he is not off God's hook, and He will deal with them. When we release the wrongdoer to God, we are not excusing his actions; we are just forgiving him as an act of obedience to God. Don't expect your feelings to help you. You have to do it as an act of your will, and you may have to do it by faith. Often our feelings will fall in line after we do the right thing. Today, God is calling you to a higher level of faith, obedience, and reward. "Let us not get tired of doing what is right, for after a while we will reap a harvest of blessing if we don't get discouraged and give up"! (Gal. 6:9 TLB).

Take a Break

If you have been mistreated, forgive the person who mistreated you. Take a moment to pray for them right now.

Endnotes

[1] *Webster's New World College Dictionary,* 3d. ed., (New York: Macmillan, 1997 Simon & Schuster), s.v. "persevere."

Prayer of Salvation

God loves you—no matter who you are, no matter what your past. God loves you so much that He gave His one and only begotten Son for you. The Bible tells us that "...whoever believes in him shall not perish but have eternal life" (John 3:16). Jesus laid down His life and rose again so that we could spend eternity with Him in heaven and experience His absolute best on earth. If you would like to receive Jesus into your life, say the following prayer out loud and mean it from your heart.

Heavenly Father, I come to You admitting that I am a sinner. Right now, I choose to turn away from sin, and I ask You to cleanse me of all unrighteousness. I believe that Your Son, Jesus, died on the cross to take away my sins. I also believe that He rose again from the dead so that I might be forgiven of my sins and made righteous through faith in Him. I call upon the name of Jesus Christ to be the Savior and Lord of my life. Jesus, I choose to follow You and ask that You fill me with the power of the Holy Spirit. I declare that right now I am a child of God. I am free from sin and full of the righteousness of God. I am saved in Jesus' name. Amen.

If you prayed this prayer to receive Jesus Christ as your Savior for the first time, please contact us on the Web at **www.harrisonhouse.com** to receive a free book.

Or you may write to us at

Harrison House
PO Box 35035
Tulsa, Oklahoma 74153

Please include your prayer requests and comments when you write.

About the Author

J. M. Farro, gifted writer and author, reaches out to thousands of people through www.jesusfreakhideout.com. Since 1996, this popular web site has grown in scope and outreach beyond the boundaries of the Christian music industry. Their focus is album reviews, artist information, interviews, music news, and ministry through devotionals and prayer. On staff since 1998, J. M. Farro counsels thousands of men and women around the globe each year through her devotionals and prayer ministry. She and her husband, Joe, have two sons. They make their home in Nazareth, Pennsylvania.

To contact J.M. Farro, please write to:
J. M. Farro
PO Box 434
Nazareth, PA 18064

Or contact by email at:
farro@jesusfreakhideout.com
or jmf@jmfarro.com

*Please include your prayer requests
and comments when you write.*

Play Dates. Birth Dates. First Dates.

Let's face it – we live our lives "on the go." However, God wants us to experience true "life." Now you can take God's words of life wherever you go. The *Life on the Go Devotional for Moms* is packed full of meaningful devotionals, stories, Scriptures, humor, and prayers that will bring purpose and richness to your fast-paced life.

With the *Life on the Go Devotional for Moms,* mothers everywhere can find time to receive from God in the middle of their busy days. Being a mom offers a lifetime of fulfilling moments. What's amazing is that in those special moments God desires to speak to us, if we will just take a moment to listen.

Life on the Go Devotional for Moms
1-57794-805-X

Available at bookstores everywhere
or visit **www.harrisonhouse.com**.

You've graduated and you're going out into the world. You are packing and leaving for the next big transition in your life. From classes and hanging out with your friends to interviews and work—it's a fast-paced world, and we are running a constant race of cell phones, computers, Web sites, magazines, coffee shops, meetings, late nights, and early mornings all while trying to fit God in. But are we doing a good job?

Let's face it – we live our lives "on the go." However, God wants us to experience true "life." Now you can take God's words of life wherever you go. The *Life on the Go Devotional for Graduates* is packed full of meaningful devotionals and stories that will bring purpose and richness to your fast-paced life. Full of Scriptures, prayers, stories, and humor; you will be charged with these unique insights and encouragements from other grads that have "been there."

Life on the Go Devotional for Graduates
1-57794-806-8

www.harrisonhouse.com

Fast. Easy. Convenient!

- ◆ New Book Information
- ◆ Look Inside the Book
- ◆ Press Releases
- ◆ Bestsellers
- ◆ Free E-News
- ◆ Author Biographies

- ◆ Upcoming Books
- ◆ Share Your Testimony
- ◆ Online Product Availability
- ◆ Product Specials
- ◆ Order Online

For the latest in book news and author information, please visit us on the Web at www.harrisonhouse.com. Get up-to-date pictures and details on all our powerful and life-changing products. Sign up for our e-mail newsletter, *Friends of the House,* and receive free monthly information on our authors and products including testimonials, author announcements, and more!

Harrison House—
Books That Bring Hope, Books That Bring Change

The Harrison House Vision

Proclaiming the truth and the power

Of the Gospel of Jesus Christ

With excellence;

Challenging Christians to

Live victoriously,

Grow spiritually,

Know God intimately.